www.theguitarexplorium.com

GW00481899

BOOK

OF

KNOWLEDGE

INTRODUCTION

Hello! And the warmest of welcomes to you. Thank you for picking up the 'Book of Knowledge' and in return for your kindness I will show you everything that I consider you MUST know on the guitar to be able to 'musician' with the best of them.

Be forewarned though, this is quite a comprehensive journey you are about to undertake and such journeys should proceed with caution and over time. This book contains potentially years of information for a beginner and, if you dive in too far too quickly, you **will** get lost and things will not make sense.

Even if you have been playing a while I'd recommend you still start at the beginning as I have structured the book in a way that it builds upon previously learned information chapter by chapter. Very few chapters stand alone and I make a lot of connections early on in an as-you-go fashion, therefore information can easily become disjointed if you skip or miss a section.

Note: There will be times in this book where I ask you to create backing tracks and hopefully record your own playing. This isn't absolutely necessary but will help considerably with your progress. Think of these like practical tests. You now need to record a backing track - can you? Are you good enough yet? Can you string the chords together without breaking the rhythm? That kind of thing. If you move forward without being able to do the above then you'll be moving too fast. However, if due to technological impairments you can't record yourself, at the very least you will need to source backing tracks from the internet or from the Guitar Explorium website to play along with.

There are also a lot of songs referenced within that you should also try and play along with as you progress. They are a variety of popular tunes that are easily found for free on internet music and video sites. They are there to encourage you to play actual music as the more music you engage with the faster you will progress.

So, are you ready? Guitar in hand? Wind in your hair?

Awesome!

Lets go...!

PARTS OF A GUITAR

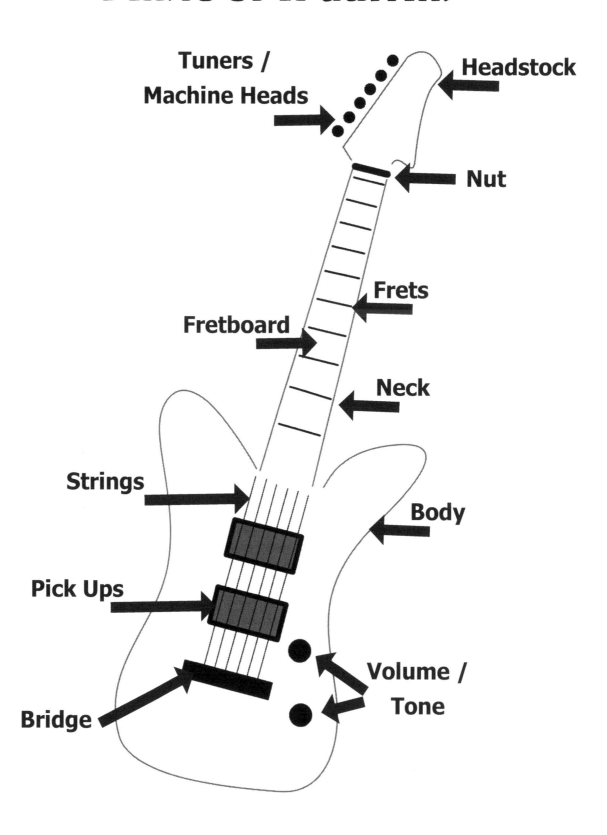

Tuners /
Machine Heads

Headstock

Nut

Frets

Fretboard

Neck

Strings

Body

Pick Ups

Volume /
Tone

Bridge

HOW TO READ!

Oh good you're still here. I did wonder how many would show up after that introduction. Anyway, we use lots of diagrams when learning guitar; Chord diagrams, scale diagrams, fretboard diagrams and tablature. At first glance they can look a little complicated but with a bit of use they soon become as natural looking as puppies who wear coats…. Um, anyway…

Naming Conventions

On guitar there are a few naming conventions to get used to. Firstly we number our strings from 1 to 6. Our 'First' string (1st) is the thinnest string on the guitar. Providing you are holding your guitar in a conventional manner, this will be the string closest to your feet. We then name the strings counting up the guitar until we reach the 6th string, the thickest string - which should be the one closest to your head.

We also name our frets (the metal bits of wire running across the neck) in a similar fashion, with the one closest to the headstock being our 1st fret and moving along the fretboard for however many you have (it can vary). However, more importantly, when we think about finger placement we actually consider the space **behind** the fret to be the figurative fret. So if I say put your finger on the first fret I mean for you to put your finger in the space **behind** the first fret rather than on the bit of metal itself - not being sarcastic, you'd be surprised.

Name your fingers!

No disrespect if you already have names for your fingers but for this book we're going to call them by number designations. This is how we're going to name your fretting hand.

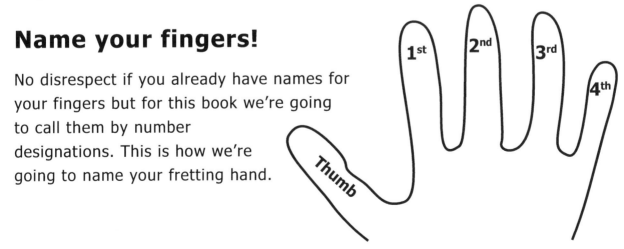

How to Read a Chord Diagram

This is a chord diagram:

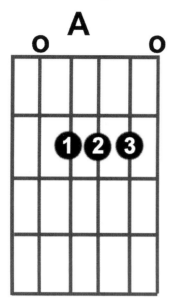

As we will discover later, this is an A chord. We know because that's the name at the top of the diagram. The 'grid' is actually an arrangement of your strings - the lines running from top to bottom, and your frets - the lines running from side to side across the strings. The black dots show us upon which string/fret we're going to place our fingers, and which finger to use is designated by the number on the black dot.

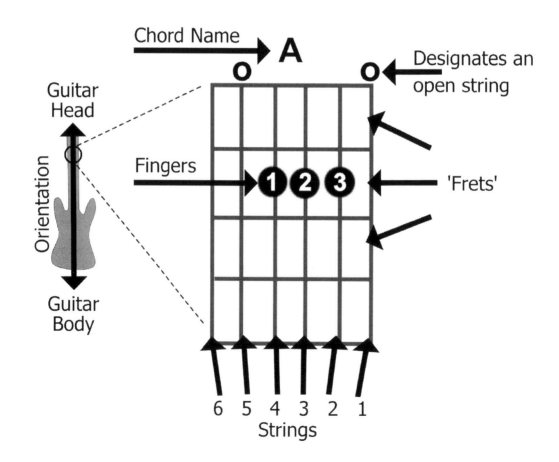

How to Read a Scale Diagram

This is a scale diagram…

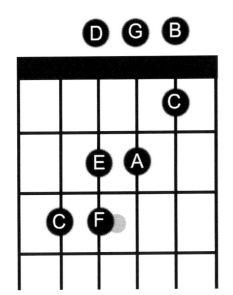

We read these in a similar fashion to the chord diagram. It is orientated the same way around as the chord diagram, the strings and frets are indicated in the same way and the dots represent where we put our fingers in a similar fashion. But instead of which finger to use the dot may notate the musical note or scale degree you get when it's played.

Also with scales we don't play all the notes at once - although feel free to try! - and therefore these dots aim to show the 'shape' of a scale, which can become a useful visualisation tool.

With some '**open position**' scales - those that use open strings as part of the scale - it's also possible for some of the notes to be indicated by dots outside of the fretboard where the notes would be if fretted by a finger.

Important: Because these diagrams only act as a visual aid they cannot explain how to play the scale, which is why these diagrams are frequently accompanied by tablature…

How to Read Tablature

Tablature is the alternative to 'reading dots' (traditional music notation) for guitar players. Although you will notice that the 'dots' are still present here. This is because whilst we don't need to read the **notes** of the traditional notation we may want to refer to the **timing** and **length of notes**.

How to read it...

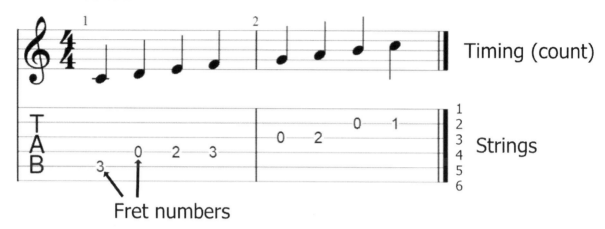

We'll focus on the section with TAB written down the left hand side. This time the horizontal lines indicated our strings. Notice that our thinnest string, the 1st string, is at the top of the diagram. This can be confusing to some as it can make the diagram appear upside down - if this is you, bear with it, as by the end of the book I'll will have completely changed your perception of reality. If this looks normal to you, then welcome to the Matrix.

The numbers on the strings indicate what frets we're going to play. In the example above there is a '3' on our 5th string to indicate that we will play the 3rd fret of our 5th string. If there is a '0' that will indicate that the string is played 'open', our '0' fret, if you like. We read it left to right and play one note at a time as we go. Generally speaking tablature doesn't indicate what fingers to use, this comes with practice and finger organisation, however if it's a particularly tricky piece you may occasionally find fingering numbers underneath the tab (but probably not, do you know how much extra work that is?!)

As mentioned, the traditional notation part of the diagram we will use only as a timing reference and we will learn to read it as we progress.

How to Read Fretboard Diagrams

Fretboard diagrams are displayed the same way as scale diagrams but cover much larger portions of the fretboard. We use these to show how the smaller shapes in our scale diagrams will connect with other shapes to form a bigger picture of your fretboard.

This diagram is all the notes of your Major and Natural minor scale covering your entire fretboard that we're going to learn in this book. But I guess you could just learn this now and we need not go on...

...well, thanks for coming, have a safe journey home...!

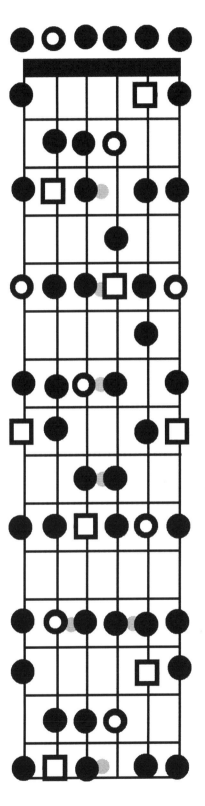

FIRST CHORDS

A, D AND E CHORDS

Ok, let not jump the gun too fast and maybe start with some chords. Let's start with our A, D and E chords. These are **Major** chords. **Major** chords are generally considered to have a positive or happy sound. Any chord that is designated by just a single letter designation is a **Major** chord.

Now might be a good time to refresh the 'How to read chords' section on page 8.

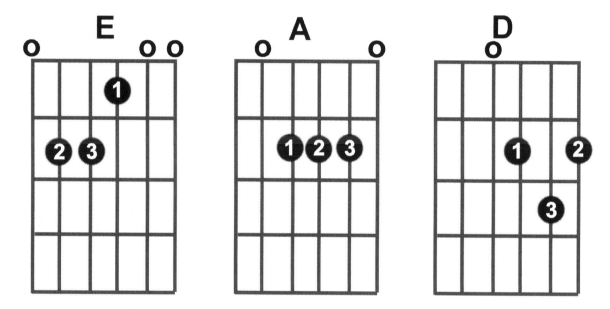

When strumming these chords its good to pay attention to the lowest open string which, as coincidence would have it for these chords, is also the name of the chord.

The E chord is played from the 6th string which is our E string.

The A chord is played from the 5th string or the A string.

And the D chord is played from the 4th string which is the D string.

The note that is also the name of the chord we call the **Root** note of the chord.

Play them with one smooth motion from the Root note all the way across all of the strings. We call this a strum.

Things to watch out for...

When playing chords there are some fundamental things to watch out for. The two most common problems you may get are **buzzing** and **dead notes**.

If your chord sounds 'funny' in either of the above ways the simplest way to determine where the problem is is to pick through the notes of the chord one string at a time until you find either the dead note or buzzy note.

If your note is 'buzzy' then it's most likely due to poor contact between the finger and the fretboard. To rectify this you can try moving your finger closer to the front or 'body side' of the fret as notes are easier to play here and harder to play from the back or 'Headstock side' of the fret. Really, try it. You will find that you need to push

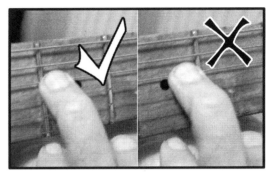

Right handed guitar pictured

harder the further to the back of the fret your finger is. With some chords like the A chord your fingers will naturally stagger across the fret, there is nothing you can do about this, just bear it in mind as a general rule. If you can't move any closer to the fret in front, or you still have a problem then it could be simply you are not pressing hard enough.

Although the solution to this isn't always 'just push harder', technique can play a large role too. Make sure the finger doing the pushing is nicely arched at it's first joint. The straighter this joint the harder it will be to push on the string.

If your note is completely dead or 'thuddy' then it could also be that another finger is obstructing the string you're playing. To correct this you need to check each other finger and check they are not touching any string other than the one they're supposed to. If you find a finger that is obstructing then you need to create bigger finger arches so each finger can reach over the other strings so as to press only the strings they are supposed to.

First Chord Progressions

Lets put these three chords together in a sequence, or **chord progression**. We're going to strum each chord 4 times and then change to the next chord.

I've written them like this:

↓ = down strum
A, D, E = the chord
/ = strum previous chord again

Try this one:

> **Down Strum**
> Strum from the lowest note of the chord across all other strings in a downward motion.

↓↓↓↓ etc

| A / / / | D / / / | E / / / | A / / / |

When changing between A and D keep your 3rd finger anchored to the neck and slide it over to form the first note of the D chord (fig 1.). This same technique can be applied to the change between D and E. Keep your 1st finger anchored to the neck and slide it into the E position. (Fig 2.)

Fig 1.

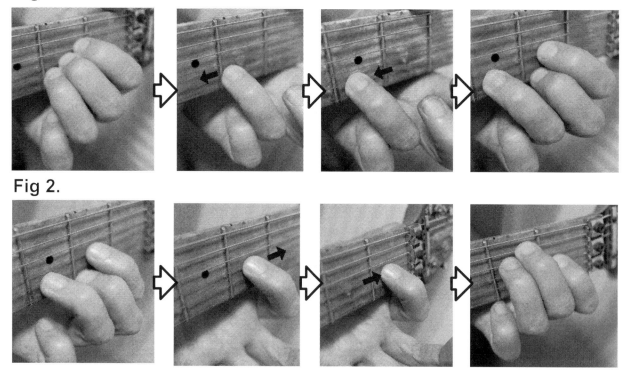

Fig 2.

Use the E to D anchor to speed up the change:

| A / / / | E / / / | D / / / | E / / / |

And the A to D anchor:

↓↓↓↓
| A / / / | D / / / | A / / / | E / / / |

And when things get a bit trickier they could really help:

↓↓↓↓
|| A / / / | A / / / | D / E / | D / E / |

Here are some song examples to look up and try:

The Cross by Prince
Wild Thing by The Troggs
Hollywood Nights by Bob Seger
Lay Down Sally by Eric Clapton
Rock n Roll by Led Zeppelin
Promised Land by Elvis Presley
Cover of the Rolling Stone by Dr Hook
Chasing Cars - Snow Patrol

Rhythm and Changing chord

As you play these focus on keeping your rhythm consistent throughout. i.e. the time between strums should be the same. Changing chord may break your rhythm to start with and you may find that can play good chords but not change from chord to chord well. This is fine. I would actually practice chords and rhythm separately. Make sure you've got good clean chords and practice changing from one to the next slowly. But also practice focusing on the rhythm only and keeping fluid time, and if you fumble the chord on the change, don't worry, keep playing, the chords will come as long as you're practising them.

C and G Chords

Theses chords are generally considered harder than our previous chords due to the stretch required to play them.

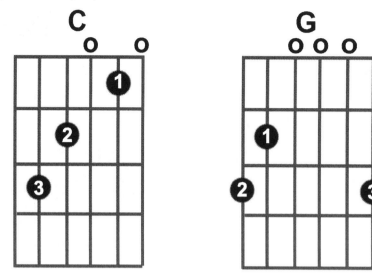

The C chord can be particularly tricky because each finger, if not arched nicely, can touch and mute the string below it. So when you strum through it check your 3rd finger isn't touching your 4th string, check your 2nd finger isn't touching your 3rd string and likewise your 1st finger isn't interfering with the open 1st string.

The Root note of the C chord is the 5th string 3rd finger - that is a C note.

The Root note for the G chord is the 6th string 2nd finger - that is a G note.

Adding the C and G

Here are some songs where we can add the C and G into our A, D and E chords. They have pretty strong rhythms so strum what you hear and don't worry too much about 'getting it wrong'. We'll look at rhythms in more detail soon, right now, just have some fun!

Songs to research:
Mull of Kintyre by Wings
Highway to Hell by ACDC
Get Back by the Beatles

A Minor Thing

Minor chords are considered our 'sad' chords because they have a more melancholy sound to them. We write their name with a small 'm' to distinguish them from our Major chords. i.e Am.

This is our A **minor** chord:

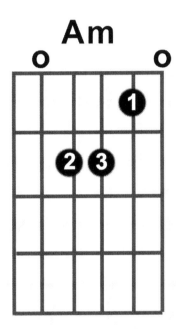

If you think about it in relation to the A Major chord, you'll notice that the note on the 2nd string has move back 1 fret. This is the note that gives it the '**minor**' sound. As with our A Major chord the **Root** note is still the open A string.

You may also notice that it's now the same 'shape' as our E Major chord, it's just moved down a string, and so the fingering is the same as it was for E Major

This chord works well next to the C Major chord.

| Am / / / | C / / / | G / / / | D / / / |

Also try these:

I only want you by Queens of the Stone Age

Shake it off by Taylor Swift

Knocking on Heavens Door by Bob Dylan

Dm and Em chords

Next we have our D minor and E minor chords. With each take the time to notice how each chord has been changed from it's Major counterpart. You will notice in both cases one note has been moved back 1 fret to create the minor sound. In the case of the E minor that note is now an open string. For the D minor chord we now have to change the fingering to accommodate the new shape. With the E minor however, you could keep the fingering the same as the E chord, just remove your 1st finger, or finger it as the diagram suggests.

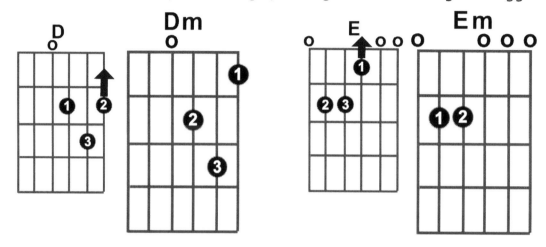

Here are some practice progressions to try:

And try this:

Ok, so with just these chords you can now play a bunch of songs. There are too many to list here and I risk copyright infringement it I write them out in too much detail! However, here are some songs that you may want to look up and try for yourself:

Picture to Burn by Taylor Swift
Wish you were here by Pink Floyd

COUNTING AND KEEPING TIME

AND A 1...2...3...4

Counting and timing are crucial skills to develop as a musician regardless of instrument. The vast majority of music has a pulse of some description that requires to be followed for the band to play together or 'in time'.

For our first adventures into the world of timing we're going to look at strumming patterns. For guitarists our strumming hand is our most natural beat keeper, closely followed by our foot or our heads!

Up until now we're been strumming in groups of 4's and everything has been a downward strum, like this:

$$| \downarrow \downarrow \downarrow \downarrow |$$

Count: 1 2 3 4

But now we're going to include up strums (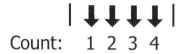) :

$$| \downarrow \uparrow \downarrow \uparrow \downarrow \uparrow \downarrow \uparrow |$$

The thing to notice is that we're not going to change the speed or '**tempo**' of our down strums but we're going to squeeze the ups into the space between them.

We're also going to count these up strums with the word 'and' - I shall abbreviate it to the symbol '&' .

So:

$$| \downarrow \uparrow \downarrow \uparrow \downarrow \uparrow \downarrow \uparrow |$$

...is counted:

Count: 1 & 2 & 3 & 4 &

Remember that you need to find a tempo where you are comfortable with strumming a strong downbeat rhythm and then add the up strums in between the downs without changing tempo. Try practising them by alternating them:

Count: 1   2   3   4   1 & 2 & 3 & 4 &

Later on we will see rhythms written like this:

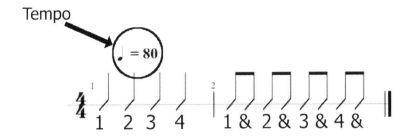

But don't panic the principle is just the same!

And a 1...2...3...

So sometimes we won't just be counting in 4's. Whilst most songs do keep to 4 beats in a bar there are lots of times when a 3 count is preferred, particularly in ballads or waltzes. On sheet music you'll see it written like: $\frac{3}{4}$

We count them exactly the same way as our 4 beats, but we obviously stop at 3 instead!

It 'feels' a lot different though so worth practising.

Good examples of songs in $\frac{3}{4}$ time are:

Mull of Kintyre by Wings

Times they are a changing by Bob Dylan

Kiss from a Rose by Seal

However, to start with, to make sure you can 'feel' how 3 sounds I would recommend you playing the root note for the first beat followed by two strums of the chord. Now this may sound a little 'country' playing it this way. But it'll help you get the 'feel'.

So for instance on the A chord we'll play the 5th string open (the A note), and then strum the rest of the chord as normal on beats 2 and 3. Then for D we'll play the open 4th string and strum the chord and for E we'll play the open 6th string and strum - you know the **Root** notes right!? You knew that...

O = Pick open root note string
↓ = strum whole chord

STRUMMING PATTERNS

Let's try some different strumming patterns, use any chords you like or just one chord as you get used to the patterns.

We'll start easy:

4 down strums:

Count: 1 2 3 4

:|| Indicates at the end of the bar to go back to the start and repeat or **loop** the pattern.

Strum every down and up:

Count: 1 & 2 & 3 & 4 &

So far so familiar.

How about missing the '&' on 1 and 4:

1   2 & 3 & 4

Remember to allow the space for the '&' after 4 before repeating back to 1.

If we keep the '&' after 4 be sure to watch the timing as you repeat back to the 1.

| ↓   ↓   ↓   ↓ ↑ :||
1   2   3   4 &

Repeat this keeping a smooth transition between 4 & 1 i.e. 1 2 3 **4 & 1** 2 ..etc

Lets add another up to make it more difficult:

| ↓↑↓ ↓ ↓↑:||
1 & 2 3 4 &

How about this:

1   2 & 3 4 &

The more you repeat this the more sense it should make!

24

Or this:

| ↓↑↓ ↓↑↓ :||
1 & 2   3 & 4

Remember to watch the rhythm as you loop them, try and avoid pausing awkwardly between them to keep a smooth rhythm - 1 & 2 & 3 & 4 **& 1** & 2 etc. Sometimes that 'going around again' can throw up the trickiest moments so keep a solid rhythm and practice getting from the 4 back to the 1.

Once you've got the hang of those you can string any arrangement of down and up strums together as you see fit. You could even string two bars together with different rhythms:

| ↓ ↓↑↓ ↓↑|↓↑↓ ↓ ↓↑:||
1   2 & 3 4 & 1 & 2 3 4 &

Experiment with some of your own ideas and go back to some earlier songs and try them with new rhythms.

Learn to stomp!

The thing about keeping time is it's quite hard to do without a reference tempo. When listening to music you are probably able to tap along with the beat without too much trouble, but when you have to keep your own time whilst strumming things can become a bit more difficult. You can get a metronome to help with this, and it's worth picking one up, but at first they can seem a little removed from the 'feel' of the song. This is why musicians learn to stomp!

Stomping is the art of stamping your foot in time to the music or, in the absence of music, is used as your inbuilt bodily metronome. But just like everything you have to practice it. So when you're counting your rhythms you should also be stomping your foot in time too. Reinforce this when listening to other music by stomping your foot along to that too and in no time your will develop a better sense of rhythm, and a metronomic leg!

Squeezing, damping and Chukkas

Sometimes when we play chords we don't want them to ring out after we play them. Sometimes we want them to be cut short and only heard on specific beats, to achieve this we need to learn to control the sound we play after we strum the chord. Enter squeezing, damping and chukkas!

Let's talk about '**squeezing**'. We do this to keep our strums shorter. It's simply the motion of, when you strum, you press down the chord with your fretting hand and once you've stopped the strum you relax your fingers reducing the pressure between fretting fingers and strings which will 'kill' the sound of the chord. So the action feels like you're squeezing the chord in time with your strumming rhythm. By squeezing the strings in this manner we can control the length of time a chord rings out which can be useful if you want to create some space and silence between your strums.

Try the simple 4 down strumming exercise:

1 & 2 & 3 & 4 &

But this time, conscious of the up strum on the '&' that we're **not** playing, use the squeezing technique to quieten the chord on the '&' beat. So strum and squeeze on 1, release pressure on '&', squeeze and strum on 2 etc. After a while it should feel quite comfortable, as your fretting hand will now be squeezing the same rhythm in time with the strumming hand and you will be creating quiet space between the beats.

Damping or **Palm muting** is a technique by which we use the fleshy part of the palm, the bit underneath the little finger, of your strumming hand to lightly touch the strings so they don't ring out fully. It gives a nice controlled sound to the chords, especially power chords (which we will explore later) when we don't want all of our strings ringing together after we play. It can make the action of strumming a little more difficult because we have to keep our palm on the bridge of our guitar to deaden the strings thus restricting movement of our strumming hand.

Try it with an A chord. Press your strumming hand palm onto your bridge quite hard so when you strum you get a 'dead' sound on the strings and the chord doesn't ring out. Then experiment with reducing pressure with your palm until you find a firmness that suits you. You should have a mostly clean chord but without it ringing out fully.

Chukkas takes damping to a whole new level. This is basically a combination of both of the previous techniques. But instead of hearing the chord we want nothing but string noise - no discernible musical noise from it whatsoever, only a 'chukk'.

Let's practice some!

For our chukka's exercise we're going to play our chord on 1, but on the '2' we're going to release all pressure on the chord **but keep your fingers on it** so when we strum it again we get just string noise designated by the **X**. The palm muting is less important with this technique. You can add it if you want a really dead chukk, but frequently the damping of the chord is enough.

You can get some cool percussive rhythms going with this technique. Try this 2 bar example:

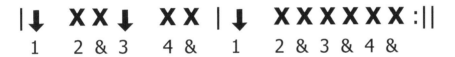

This is a pretty popular technique in funk and its peripheral styles but can also be heard frequently in punk, rock and metal.

Nirvana's 'Smells like Teen Spirit' is a good example of chukkas and the Verse from 'By the way' by the Red Hot Chilli Pepper is a fine example of 'chukk-ing' to the max!

SCALES

DOH REY ME...

Doh Rey Me... remember that? That's how old people like me were taught the concept of scales at school... I personally didn't understand it to be honest, although I do now, but I have had 40 years to process it!

So what is a scale?

Before we answer that I want to show you all our available notes. We have 12 available notes A-G, once we get to G we go back to A, I guess at that point the naming committee decided to call it a day and went home, because A-G is all we have! 'But that's only 7 notes!' I hear you exclaim, 'You owe me 5 notes!'. And you'd be right. There are some hidden notes too. If you look on a piano keyboard and see the white notes, they are the notes, alphabetically, A - G. The black notes are the 'in-between' notes - you know, the notes that when you play them sound horrible so you decide not to and stick with just the white ones? (maybe that was just me). There are 5 black notes and they are **en-harmonic** notes. Which just means they have two names depending on how you describe them - either sharp (#) or flat (♭).

I'll count all 12 notes out here for you:

A	A#/B♭	B	C	C#/D♭	D	D#/E♭	E	F	F#/G♭	G	G#/A♭	A
1	2	3	4	5	6	7	8	9	10	11	12	1

12 Notes. If this was a scale we'd call it a **chromatic** scale, because we've played every note. But most of what we'll be doing is going to be either a Major scale or a minor scale.

To describe a Major scale we use a formula consisting of whole steps and half steps. This basically means for a **W**hole step we jump 2 places and for a **H**alf step we jump 1. Anyway, our Major scale formula goes like this: W W H W W W H .

Then all we do is apply that to our sequence of notes above and we get a Major scale. So if we start from A (please follow along!) we would get the notes :

A   B   C#   D   E   F#   G#   (A)

W   W   H   W   W   W   H

These notes would equal an A Major scale. But ugh! Look at all those horrible sharps!

Let's do it from C instead...

```
C   D   E   F   G   A   B   (C)
W   W   H   W   W   W   H
```

That's better. So our C Major scale has the notes C D E F G A and B.

Just to confuse exactly what we just did we're now going to name each of these notes with an interval number - basically something that tells us what number each note in the scale it is. So:

```
C  D  E  F  G  A  B  C
1  2  3  4  5  6  7  1
```

This is where our Doh Rey Me came from at school, instead of singing notes, we were singing interval numbers:

```
Doh  Rey  Mee  Far  So  Lar  Tee  Doh
 1    2    3    4    5    6    7    1
```

However, I'm not going to mention this method again, we're all grown up here so proper notes only from now on!

If we have a quick look at minor scales they work much the same but the formula is different- W H W W H W W

So a C minor scale would be:

```
C    D    E♭   F    G    A♭   B♭   C
W    H    W    W    H    W    W
```

A useful thing we can do with the minor scale is to compare it to the Major scale:

```
Major scale    C    D    E    F    G    A    B    C
               1    2    3    4    5    6    7    1

Minor scale    C    D    E♭   F    G    A♭   B♭   C
               1    2   ♭3    4    5   ♭6   ♭7    1
```

From this we can see that both scales are the same except the minor scale has a ♭3, ♭6 and ♭7.

This may seem like information of which one doesn't care much at the moment, but oh my, you will... oh yes... indeed.... you will.... Mwahahahahaha....

Ahem... Excuse that outburst.

In fact you have already seen that minor scale at work in your minor chords. Lets look at your two A chords:

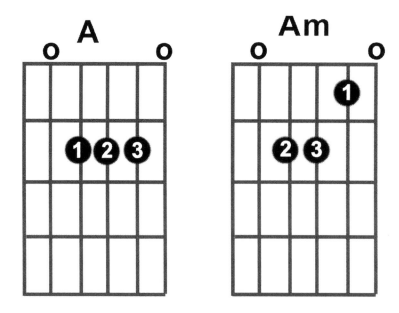

See how that one note is different between them? Well, that's the third, in the A chord that note is a C#, in the A minor chord its a C. That's because in a minor scale we have a flat third.

A Major scale: A   B   C#   D   E   F#   G#

A minor scale: A   B   C   D   E   F   G

Just to put your mind at ease somewhat, you won't need to do this stuff yourself, I put it here for those who like to have all the information... The same people who like to fold their socks in pairs... You know the type!

By the way, have you noticed how the A minor scale has the same notes as a C Major scale?

Hmmmm....

THE C MAJOR SCALE

As explained in the previous chapter, this is a Major scale starting from the note C:

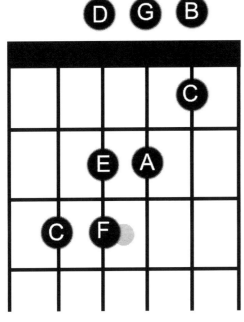

For those with the deduction skill of Batman, you will recognise this scale from the How to Read section - if you did you get bonus points - I'm keeping count you know.

Use the TAB to play the scale and the diagram to learn the note names. The tab is in alphabetical order from C to C, so just call out the notes as you play them.

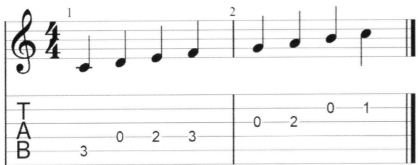

A note on fingering

To become a 'master of fingers', playing this scale a 'finger-a-fret' is great practice.

So place your 1st, 2nd, and 3rd fingers over their corresponding frets and play the scale that way. i.e. start with your 3rd finger and play the 3rd fret 5th string. The next string is open so no finger is necessary, but the next one you will play with your 2nd finger because it's the 2nd fret of the 4th string. The next you'll use your 3rd finger because it's the 3rd fret etc... So as well as showing you the frets to play you can also use the same numbers to indicate which finger to use.

OPEN POSITION NOTE NAMES

Now, just knowing the scale is great an all, but to really bleed all the information possible from it we're going to view it in a couple of different ways.

Firstly we want to name all the notes. This is easy, because with C Major its just a case of reciting your alphabet: C D E F G A B which brings you back to C.

Knowing these notes in open position is really useful because it now gives you a starting point for knowing the note names in your open chords... and this is good because we'll need them later.

However, when we play a scale we don't have to restrict ourselves to starting at C and finishing at C, we can also play those notes anywhere on the fretboard in any position, so lets have a look at completing this 'open position' C Major scale by filling in all other scale notes:

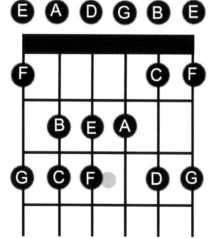

This is all our notes in C Major in our open position. It contains only the notes of C Major from lowest note (E) to highest note (G) in 'Open Position'.

Here's the full position in Tab form in case you find that easier to read:

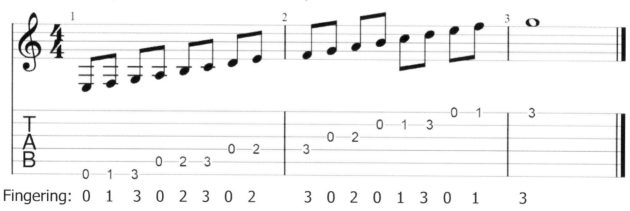

Fingering: 0 1 3 0 2 3 0 2   3 0 2 0 1 3 0 1   3

If I can refer you back to the Doh Rey Me chapter once more, you'll remember how most of our notes had whole steps between them, leaving room for a sharp (♯) or flat (♭). You can see that in action here. You'll notice between our F to G there is a unused fret. This is our F♯ or G♭ note. It's not in our current scale but it's there. Likewise between our open D and our E there is room for a D♯ or E♭ at our 1st fret. Hopefully you get the idea.

So for instance, if you wanted to really test yourself, you could make an A chord and try and figure out the notes in that chord. You have 2nd fret notes on your 4th, 3rd and 2nd string. You now know that on your 4th string that note is an E, on your 3rd string its an A, and we can work out that on our 2nd string its the note between a C and a D, in this case we'll call it C♯.

It's that easy!

Ok, I'll cut you a bit of slack, it does takes a little bit of familiarity and getting used to, and in all honesty you don't *need* to be able to do this, but it's these concepts and little bits of fretboard knowledge like this that will really bring your playing together later on. Plus knowing notes on the guitar neck is pretty showy offy when you talk to other guitar players and actually name notes. Just watch their jaws drop!

Quick Note:

Throughout the book you will notice I capitalise the M on the word Major and don't on the word minor. This is a little brain game I like to play to enable you to recognise the difference between Major and minor just at a glance. Outside of chord naming etiquette this isn't actually a music theory concept - this is just how I like to present information.

G MAJOR OPEN POSITION

While we're in the mood for scales, lets do 1 more. This will be the last one (for now).

Lets do our open G Major scale:

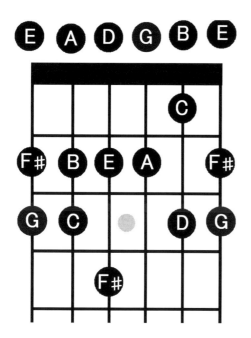

Wait it's fine! Come back!! It's ok, don't be afraid... take a deep breath and lets try again...

What if I told you that your G Major scale is the same as your C Major scale except for 1 note, would that make you feel better?!

Let's look at the diagram again and let's read the notes: We have G A B C D E and F#. Those are the same notes as our C Major scale except with an F# instead of an F note.

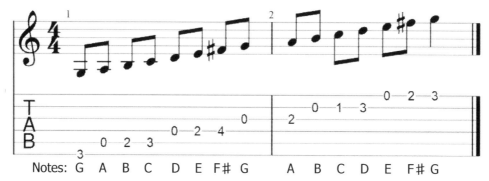

Notes: G A B C D E F# G   A B C D E F# G

You will have noticed that I've given the entire 1st position for this scale, which was a little unfair, but for now lets just play the notes in order from G on the 6th string to the open G string (3rd string). You should be able to hear that familiar 'Major sound', the Doh Rey Me sound. Compare it to the C Major scale and notice how they sound 'the same' but at the same time are different. This is because the **intervals** between the notes are consistent in each scale, so you're ears are learning to recognise the concept of musical intervals. Cool huh!

Now continue the journey by playing the open G to the 1st string G, again it sounds the same, you can hear the Major tonality. Each one of those G to G's we call an **Octave** because each has eight notes. Now play the whole scale listening out for those Major tonalities.

A note on picking

While you're practising these there is also something you can practice along side them, and that is your picking technique.

The bottom line is you can pick the strings however you like **but** can I propose that if you are using a pick then try alternating your pick stroke on every note.

Just as we did with strumming our rhythms, we'll use the same down / up approach when we're picking notes.

V = Down pick
^ = Up pick

Picking: V ^ V ^ V ^ V ^   etc..
             1 & 2 & 3 & 4 &

The benefits of using **alternate picking** are, once you get used to it, it's easier to play faster - it's much harder to play two consecutive down strokes than a down followed by an up.

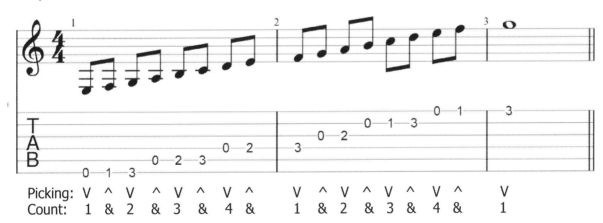

Picking: V ^ V   ^ V ^ V ^   V ^ V ^ V ^ V ^   V
Count: 1 & 2   & 3 & 4 &   1 & 2 & 3 & 4 &   1

Good job! Ok, now take a bit of a break, grab a sandwich, and I'll see you fresh and eager in the next section.

How Songs Work

WHAT IS A KEY?

When we learn to write songs it's nice to start with the idea of **chord families**. These are chords that go together and demonstrate our basic music writing concept of **tension and release.**

To do this we will consider our musical '**key**'. We've already done this in our scales chapter. Remember when we compared the C Major scale and the G Major scale and could tell they sounded the same but the notes were different. That's how a 'key' works. People choose the key of a song for different reasons. Sometimes it's the singers range that might dictate the key or sometimes the tuning of the instruments that are being played, or sometimes it can be that it's simply easier to play certain keys on guitar.

For this lesson we're going to stick to the keys of C and G.

What's a chord family?

Chord families are chords that are frequently found together and are derived from the notes of the Major scale of the key we're in.

So if we're in the key of C our notes are:

C D E F G A B

To figure out what chords are in the family we need to figure out a chord for each of those notes.

To do this we take the Root note of the chord we want, in this case we want a C chord so we start with the C note. We then add to it the 3rd note from C and the 5th note from C. That gives us the C - Root, the E - 3rd note, and G - the 5th note. That gives us a C Major chord.

C D **E** F **G** A B = CEG = C Major chord

R 2 **3** 4 **5** 6 7

We then do the same to discover our D chord.

C **D** E **F** G **A** B = DFA = D minor chord
7 **R** 2 **3** 4 **5** 6

That's D - Root, F - the 3rd, and A - the 5th. If we put those together we get a D **minor** chord. Check out your chords for D and D minor. You'll notice that the D chord has a F♯ on the 1st string, our D minor chord however has the natural F on the 1st string. We know that we want an F not F♯ so we know its the D minor chord.

Now, we could go on and do this for each chord, but I'm hoping you get the idea and the concept of this book is to give you the understanding of how it works without being too theory intensive. But don't worry about having to go through this process every time you want to find a chord family because luckily, there is a 'cheat'!

Once all our chords have been figured out we end up with the chords C Dm Em F G Am and B diminished.

So we can say the chords in the C Major chord family are:

C Dm Em F G Am Bdim

The F chord we haven't done yet, but we will in a bit - and the B diminished - well let's think of the B diminished as the member of the family that is a bit 'out there' and you don't see them very often except maybe at the holidays.

Anyway, the 'cheat' I alluded to a moment ago, is understanding that no matter what Major scale you use to figure out your chords the result will always be the same sequence of chords - **Major minor minor Major Major minor Diminished.** I actually want you to repeat that sequence until you remember it! It's going to be so very very important as we progress.

To demonstrate this idea lets take our G Major scale:

G A B C D E F♯

So the same method would apply, we can take the Root, 3rd and 5th of every note and figure out the chords or we can just apply our sequence - **M m m M M m d** - to the scale:

So G A B C D E F♯ becomes G Am Bm C D Em F♯dim

So we can say that the chords in our G Major chord family are:

G Am Bm C D Em F♯dim

Once more with a trickier one: if I told you that the note of the E Major scale were:

E F♯ G♯ A B C♯ D♯

You can ignore how horrible those note look and simply apply the same pattern and you can tell me that the Chord family is:

E F♯m G♯m A B C♯m and D♯diminished !

Major minor minor Major Major minor Diminished

Tah-dah!! Chord families with no effort!

Circle of 5th's

To learn the notes of keys you should consider studying the circle of 5ths.
I shall put it at the end of the book in it's own section, including a way we can study it specifically on guitar.

However, because right now we can get by without it we'll leave it there, however you may find it useful to look at the further we progress. So do check it out when you a) have the time and b) when you're feeling brave enough.

MISSING CHORDS

So ignoring the diminished chord, I'm aware that we haven't encountered the B minor chord from the G Major family yet or the F chord from the C Major family so lets do those here.

B minor is the easiest of the two chords even though it calls upon the use of our 4th finger, so we'll start with that one.

B minor

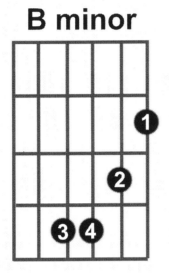

We start with your 1st finger on the 2nd fret 1st string, 2nd finger on 3rd fret 2nd string, 3rd finger on the 4th string 4th fret, and our 4th finger is placed on the 3rd string 4th fret. If you take your 1st finger out of the equation it's worth noting that your 2nd, 3rd and 4th fingers are making an Am chord shape but at the 3rd fret... interesting...

Practice with this progression:

| E / / / | Bm / / / | D / / / | A / / / :||

and try

| Bm / / / | E / / / | A / / / | D / / / :||

A great song to practice your Bm chord along to is the 4 Non Blondes song 'What's up' - check it out!

Also Mazzy Star's 'Fade Into you', is pretty cool and you get to practice counting in 3's too.

Cool, ready for the F chord?...

It may be a little harder...

Dun dun duuuuun!!

Please excuse the F's need to be overly dramatic. There's no need to let it intimidate you, it's just a case of approaching it correctly. It's all about hand position you see.

You'll notice from the diagram we have to hold down two strings with our first finger for this, which is all about position. You have two options...

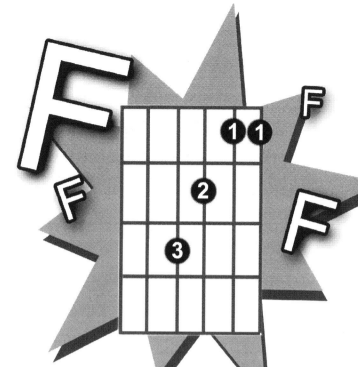

If you have a 'proper*' thumb-behind-the-neck hand position then you will probably find you need to fret the two strings slightly with the side of your 1st finger if you have a 'grabby'* thumb-over position you'll be using your fingerprint. The trick is to keep this first finger flat whilst keeping arches in fingers 2 and 3. Perseverance is key here.

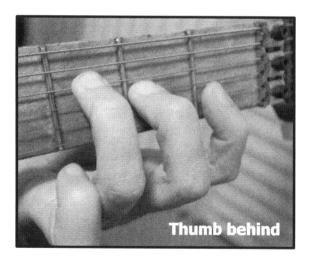

Thumb behind

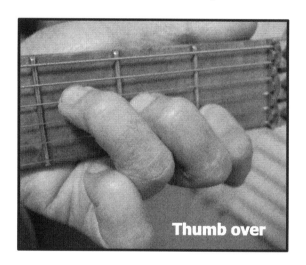

Thumb over

A nice progression to practice this is:

| F / / / | C / / / | G / / / | G / / / ||

Again, make up your own strumming patterns.

* The terms 'grabby' and 'proper' are not used to say one is better than the other, whatever is comfortable for you is the correct way.

Chord Progressions

Like many individuals within families, our chords each have a different way of communicating to each other. To understand this we're going to give our chords function names, or numbers actually.

We name them with Roman Numerals so as not to confuse them with other numerical system that we have going on, and we're going to consider our Root chord number 'I', and number the rest sequentially from there:

C Dm Em F G Am Bdim
I   ii   iii IV V   vi   vii

Just to add a little more clarification, for the Major chords we use capital 'I's and for minor chords we use lowercase 'i's.

Dominants

We have two **Dominant** chords. The V chord and the IV chord. The V chord is called the **Dominant** chord and the IV chord is called the **sub dominant** chord. The terms Dominant and sub dominant come from the fact that both tonic notes are a 5th away from the root - the Dominant is a 5th higher than the root and the sub dominant is a 5th lower than the root. However, this is a bit too 'music theory' than I want to get in to in this book, but if you're interested I'm sure a quick internet search will get you any answers you may seek!

Our V chord is probably the most well know chord after the Root (I) chord. As discussed, the V chord we call the **Dominant** chord and it likes to **resolve** to the Root (I) more than any other chord. We can demonstrate this by playing:

| C / / / | Em / / / | G / / / | G / / / | G / / / | G / / / |....etc | C / / / |

You will notice that the longer you hang onto that G chord the more your ear will beg you to **resolve** back to the C chord.

This **V - I** resolve is a technique used in all styles of music from classical to rock to jazz. In music theory we call this resolve a **perfect cadence**.

Our IV chord is our **Sub-dominant** chord. This too likes to resolve to the root but the 'pull' towards the root is less so because the resolving notes tend to move down, whereas with the **Dominant** chord the resolving notes move up. This results in a resolve that feels more mellow than the **perfect cadence** which feels more urgent.

| C / / / | Em / / / | F / / / | C / / / |

A much more mellow resolve, I think you'll agree. This **IV - I** resolve is called a **plagal cadence** - you know, just in case you're asked!

If we do the same for our G Major family we have:

G Am Bm C D Em F♯dim
I ii iii IV V vi vii

So our Dominant is D, that's the one that like to resolve to the Root, and the subdominant is the C.

Experiment

At this point it's worth playing with your own chord progressions for a bit. Pick a key, either C or G and play with the chords from your chosen family. Always start with the root chord and then choose some others. Maybe take 4 bars and put a new chord in each and see how they work together.

|G / / / | Em / / / | C / / / | D / / / :||
  I   vi   IV   V

Remember to experiment with putting your dominant and sub dominant into bar 4 to see how they effect the repeat, but there are no rules, just play and experiment. Don't forget to try different strumming patterns and try experimenting with different numbers of bars. 4 is nice, but maybe a little short, maybe try doing something in 8 bars.

|G / / / | G / / / | Em / / / | C / / / | D / / / |D / / / | C / / / | D / / / :||
  I   vi   IV   V   IV   V

Or you can always have two chords in a bar if your chord changes are up to it.

| G / / / | C / D / | Em / / / | C / D / :||

CAPOS ARE NOT CHEATING!

Capos are useful. Although word on the street is that 'capos are cheating'. This is simply not true as I'm sure we'll discover as we go.

Anyway, I may be getting ahead of myself...

What is a Capo?

A capo is a device that bars a fret on your neck to allow you to consider the open string position higher up on your fretboard.

I'm here to help

For instance if you put a capo on your neck at the 2nd fret and played an open C chord it would musically be a D chord but you could still treat it like a C chord and likewise all your chords in your C Major chord family would remain relative to each other in the capo's position - even though you'd now technically be playing in the key of D Major.

i.e. you'd be playing the chords shapes: C Dm Em F G Am Bdim

                                            I   ii   iii IV V vi   vii

But the music coming out of your guitar will be: D Em F#m G A Bm C#dim

                                                I   ii   iii IV V vi   vii

And you didn't have to work out any music theory for that to happen.

And this is why we learn the number method - It's less about what the chord name is but how it sounds that's important! So if you know the chord progression as a number sequence then, if you have your capo with you, you can play it anywhere!

We're going to do a lot more of this in a very short while, so if you don't have a capo, now is a great time to pop out and get one and I'll see you back here in a bit...

THE I IV V
BLUES POWER!

Probably the most famous chord progression in Rock and Blues is the **I IV V** progression. There is simply not a list long enough that could contain all the songs written solely with these three chords. However a good place to start would be the **12 bar blues progression**, so named due to there being 12 bars.

Being a I IV V progression we can play it in any key - we'll do it in C.

Just take your I chord (C) your IV chord (F) and your V chord (G) and play this:

| C / / / | C / / / | C / / / | C / / / | F / / / | F / / / | C / / / | C / / / |
| G / / / | F / / / | C / / / | G / / / :||

There are a few variations but they're basically the same and just a case of listening out for the changes... watch your bass player!

Sometimes you'll find the same idea but over 16 bars, which we call... you guessed it... a 16 Bar Blues. That would go something like this:

| C / / / | C / / / | F / / / | F / / / | C / / / | C / / / | G / / / | G / / / |
| C / / / | C / / / | F / / / | F / / / | C / / / | G / / / | C / / / | G / / / :||

Note that both progressions end with the V chord which resolves the progression back to the I chord.

Although we've done this in C Major, that's probably one of the less likely keys you'll find a 12 bar blues in. Being a very traditional blues progression it's more probable you'll find it in 'guitar keys'. Traditionally guitarist like open strings so the keys of A and E are always more popular than C in traditional rock and blues music.

If we change it to the key of A, our chord family is:

A Bm C♯m **D E** F♯m Gdim

So our I IV V chords are: A D E

And if we did it in E Major our chord family would be: **E** F♯m G♯m **A B** C♯m D♯dim

So in E our I IV V chords are: E A and B.

Hmmm B...

B

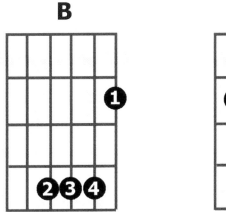

B7

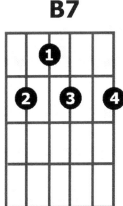

This is a B chord, just like the B minor chord it starts on the second fret and plays an 'A' shape on the 4th fret. It's a little harder than the B minor because we have more of a stretch between 1st and 2nd finger. Alternatively we can play the B7. I say alternatively because we wouldn't normally substitute a B for a B7 but because we're doing I IV V blues progressions you can use B7 as the V chord in E.

```
| E / / / | E / / / | E / / / | E / / / |
| A / / / | A / / / | E / / / | E / / / |
| B(7) / / / | A / / / | E / / / | E / / / :||
```

Some obvious song choices that use the 12 bar blues I IV V progression are:

Johnny B Goode - Chuck Berry - Actually more-or-less any Chuck Berry song uses this progression! Unfortunately he played a lot in flat keys so we won't worry for the moment but I wanted to mention him because he really did define this chord progression and that rock n roll style that was copied by so many. To get his songs in easier keys you might want to look for band covering his songs like:
Rock and Roll Music by The Beatles

Other songs worth listening to:

The Jack by AC DC
Rave on by Buddy Holly
Tush by ZZ Top
Crossroads by Cream

I IV V songs

In all honesty there are so so many songs that use the I IV V formula, I'm sure once you hear it a few times you'll be able to find your own examples.

But here are a few I IV V songs that **don't** use a strict 12 bar blues template:

The Mighty Quinn by Bob Dylan

Walk of Life by Dire Straits

Twist and Shout by The Beatles

Mmm Bop by Hanson

I Fought the Law by The Bobby Fuller Four

Cover of the Rolling Stone by Dr Hook

Check out each of these songs. Either see if you can work out the chords by listening to them - my preferred method - or find the music and play through each. Remember there are only 3 chords in each of these songs - and you know them - so how hard can it be, right?!

Getting used to playing and recognising chord progressions is such a useful tool. By doing it you are training your ears to recognise chords and intervals. Soon you'll be listening to songs and knowing the chords or intervals before you even pick up your guitar!

THE I V vi IV
POP GOES THE CHORUS

The next most used chord progression in Pop and Rock music has to be the I V vi IV progression. You're less likely to hear an entire song composed of this chord progression but they do exist - Auld Lang Syne probably being the most common example. But this progression makes a great chorus.

Lets play it first.

As usual, in the key of C we have our chord family:

C   Dm   Em   F   G   Am   Bdim
I   ii   iii IV V   vi   viii

So we can extract our I V vi IV from that to give us:

C   G   Am   F
I   V   vi   IV

All of the examples below use one chord per bar/measure such as:

| C / / / | G / / / | Am / / / | F / / / :||
  I   V   vi   IV

I'm sure just after playing that you can hear something familiar about it.

Lets do it in the key of G too:

| G / / / | D / / / | Em / / / | C / / / :||
  I   V   vi   IV

So, I'm hoping you can tell that these progressions are the same. Hearing the relationships between chords is key (no pun intended) to picking out songs by yourself.

The Return of the Capo

As promised this is where I said we'll need a capo. Lots of these songs are in key's that we haven't got the chords for yet so we're going to use the capo to get you used to the number system in the keys we do know. We're going to use two chord families the

C Major and G Major and move them with the capo if necessary.

All of the following songs use a I V vi IV progression. Your mission, should you choose to accept it, is to play along. To do this you need to figure out the first note of the first chord of the song. Do this by running your finger up your 6th string or 5th string until you find a match. Listen to the first note, sing it in your head, compare it on your fretboard, find the match. If you found the note on your 6th string, that is going to be where you play a G chord. If you need to, place your capo relative the G chord where the open strings would be. If you found the note on your 5th string, this will be your C chord. If required, place the capo next to your chord where your open strings would be. You should now be 'in key'.

With your capo on the correct fret and with your first C or G chord recognised you will continue to play the I V vi VI progression in C or G along to the song. All that will be left to do is to recognise where the song is changing chord.

Try these:

Perfect - Pink

Someone you loved - Lewis Capaldi

Perfect - Ed Sheeran

We Didn't Start the Fire - Billy Joel

Let it be - The Beatles

These last two mix the I V vi IV order up a bit more, but remain using those same 4 chords. See if you can follow the chord progression now you know what chords they're using.

Country Roads - John Denver

Friday I'm In Love - the Cure

After a while of practising this, the chord changes become quite predicable. Have patience and persevere. It's all about training your ears. You can do this!

RELATIVE MAJORS AND MINORS

You know that member of your family who you have lots in common with but they're always sad. Well chord families have those too...

Lets look at our chords in C again:

C Dm Em F G Am Bdim

We can actually pair these chords up. The sad (minor) relative chord is always 6 away from the happy (Major) one:

C's sad relative is Am - C is I, Am is vi

F's sad relative is Dm - if F were I, Dm would be vi

G's sad relative is Em - if G was I, then Em would be vi

Or you can think of the minor chord as being 3 below the Root i.e. vi-vii-I.

Am is the **relative minor** of C Major for example or C Major is the **Relative Major** of A minor

Like all healthy relationships we're going to exploit the bajeezuz out of this one as we progress, but for now lets leave it there.

THE VI IV I V
ANGSTY POP

This is basically the same chord progression as the I V vi IV, except you'll notice that the last two chords have become the first two. This is makes for a really cool device that means we can still think about our song in terms of being in a Major key but we can start with the **relative minor** chord and thus stop it sounding so blooming happy all the time!

Just for your convenience I'll repeat the keys here, even though I know you already know them off by heart by now...

C Major: C   Dm   Em   F   G   Am   Bdim
                            I   ii   iii   IV   V   vi   vii

So the vi IV I V progression is:

Am   F   C   G
vi   IV   I   V

And in G Major its:

G   Am   Bm   C   D   Em   F#dim
I   ii   iii   IV   V   vi   vii

So the vi IV I V progression is:

Em   C   G   D
vi   IV   I   V

Using the same method as before, find the root chord, use your capo if necessary, and then play along with these:

Zombie - The Cranberries
The Passenger - Iggy Pop
You're not sorry - Taylor Swift
One of us - Joan Osbourne
Should've said no - Taylor Swift

THE I vi IV V
THE 50'S PROGRESSION

This is a pretty cheesy chord progression if you play it as I'm about to demonstrate it. You can make good songs from it however, in fact it's called the '50's' progression for the very reason that around that time you couldn't throw a rock without hitting a song written with this progression. From Blue Moon to Stand by Me everyone was using it. Rather than to state them all here I will defer you to wikipedia where under the search '50's progression' you will find a long list of songs of which I refer. Lets play it.

If we play in our now favourite key of C Major:

C   Dm   Em   F   G   Am   Bdim
I   ii   iii IV V   vi   vii

We get the progression:

C   Am   F   G
I   vi   IV V

And in G Major its:

G   Am   Bm   C   D   Em   F#dim
I   ii   iii IV V   vi   vii

So the vi IV I V progression is:

G   Em   C   D
I   vi   IV V

Let me leave you with this:

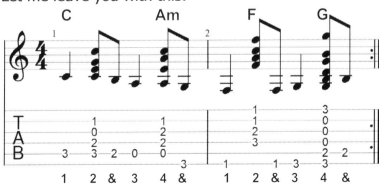

MOVING CHORDS

STRUMMING PATTERNS 2

Syncopation

Syncopation is a fancy word that means we're going to accent the up strums in our strumming patterns. We'll look at some examples at the end of the section but first lets practice playing **off the beat.**

This is our normal rhythm:

|↓ ↑ ↓ ↑ ↓ ↑ ↓ ↑|

Count: 1 & 2 & 3 & 4 &

We're going to do what we did before in our strumming exercises but this time we'll gradually take away our downbeats. Try this:

|↓ ↑ ⇩ ↑ ↓ ↑ ↓ ↑|

Count: 1 & (2) & 3 & 4 &

The secret to doing this well is to really build up a solid strumming arm action. Your arm has to be thinking like the top example **all the time.** So regardless of the strumming pattern, your arm will always continue with its constant up/down motion. You need to turn your arm into a machine!

What will happen when, as with the second example, you need to play a down beat that isn't being played you will simply miss the strings on the downbeat and hit them as usual on the up. This way your arm hasn't missed a beat, you simply missed the strings! **Do not play the up strums with down strums!**

Try this one:

|↓ ↑ ↓ ↑ ⇩ ↑ ↓ ↑|

Count: 1 & 2 & (3) & 4 &

This time we are missing the 3 beat but your strumming hand is going to 'action' all beats but miss the strings on the downbeat of 3 so the & after 3 will be played on the up strum as normal.

Missing the 3 is probably the most useful pop / rock strumming rhythm. It should definitely feel familiar to your ears once you've got it down.

Here's a more basic example of missing the 3:

| ↓   ↓↑   ⇓   ↑↓ |

Count: 1   2 & (3) & 4

This time we're also missing up strums on 1& and 4& but these shouldn't cause a problem because it's just what we were doing in our initial strumming patterns section. Once again the one to focus on is the downbeat of 3. A good tip is to count it out rhythmically first 'one, two and, and four... one, two and, and four... We'll make this our mantra for all things rhythmic from now on: **If in doubt, count it out!** Or how about: **If you can't say it, you can't play it!**

Here's a pattern that will build more syncopation:

Count: 1 & (2) & (3) & 4 &

Count it out and think of the strumming pattern: down-up,   up,   up-down-up

Count: 1 & (2) & (3) & 4 &

If we drop all the downbeats we end up with this - **but make sure you're still tapping your foot on the 1 beat!**

Popular songs with syncopated rhythms are Obladi Oblada by the Beatles or UB40's Red Red wine - you'll notice all the guitar rhythm stabs are all on the '&' beats.

Up strum except when you downstrum...

When things get so syncopated that all you're playing is the 'up' strum it's actually quite normal to play them with downstrums!... I know, I know, I teach you one thing and then there's always an exception! The fact is that you tend to get more attack with the pick during downstrums plus it's easier to mute on downstrums, so playing these 'accent' beats with a downstrum is fine - feel free to change your strumming patterns according to the needs of the song, its feel, and the required technique to get the effect you're after.

| ⇓ ↑ ⇓ ↑ ⇓ ↑ ⇓ ↑ | Or | ↓   ↓   ↓   ↓ |

(1) & (2) & (3) & (4) &   (1) & (2) & (3) & (4) &

SO, A CHORD WALKED INTO A BAR...

The two words that strike fear into the hearts of all new guitar players, Barre Chords!

You'll find two spellings for barre chords, **barre** and **bar**, they're the same thing, you can use either so don't let that confuse anything - I'll try and be consistent!

Now, barre chords have a bad reputation for being hard and, I won't dress it up for you, they are... however, it may surprise you that you've already done 3 of them, I just didn't tell you that's what you were doing.

Let's go back in time a little bit...

(wibbly wobbly time travel music)

B minor is the easiest of the two chords even though it calls upon the use of our 4th finger, so we'll start with that one.

B minor

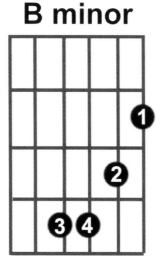

We start with your 1st finger on the 2nd fret 1st string, 2nd finger on 3rd fret 2nd string, 3rd finger on the 4th string 4th fret, and our 4th finger is placed on the 3rd string 4th fret. If you take your 1st finger out of the equation it's worth noting that your 2nd, 3rd and 4th fingers are making an Am chord shape but at the 3rd fret... interesting...

Ok, let's stop there...

Remember this?... Well, B minor is a **barre chord**, or I prefer the term **movable chord**. We consider it movable because we can move it and it becomes a new chord. For instance you can see that B minor is an A minor chord moved up two frets. We then cover what was the open string with our 1st finger:

Am   **Bm**

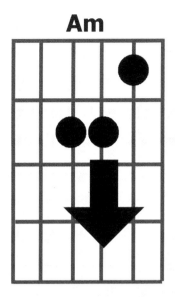

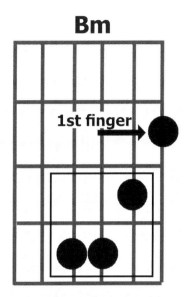

We can also keep going. If we move the B minor shape up one more fret so our 1ˢᵗ finger is on the 3ʳᵈ fret it becomes a C minor, two more frets and it becomes a D minor. We'll learn how to figure out the names for these in a bit, but for now just know that is how it's movable.

Well that's not too hard! 'So what's so tricky about bar chords?' I hear you ask. Well, as I said this is a movable chord, not strictly a barre chord... this :-

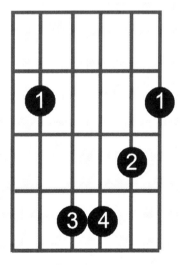

...this is a bar chord!

It's all about that 1st finger. You'll notice on the diagram we now appear to have two first fingers. It's ok, we don't need a friend for this one. It is simply indicating that our 1st finger is going to **barre** across those 5 strings from the 5th to the 1st also holding down those in-between. Because we have notes further up the fretboard on our 2nd, 3rd and 4th strings we don't show the 1st finger in those frets.

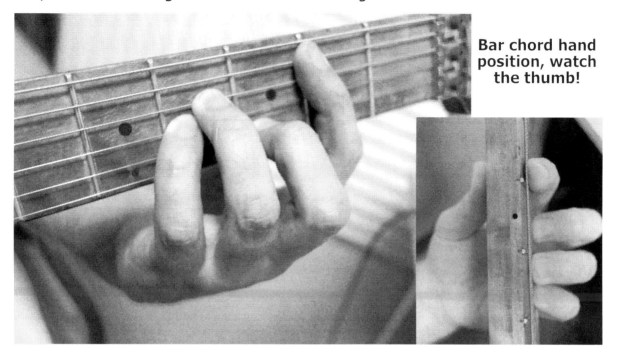

Bar chord hand position, watch the thumb!

For now we're going to split our barre chords into the 2 most popular groups - E shapes and A shapes.

Here are the two 'A Shape' barre chords. You can see the first one is an A chord moved up with a Barred 1st finger and the second is the 'Am shape' moved up and barred with first finger.

'A Shape'

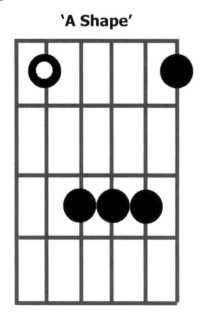

'Am Shape'

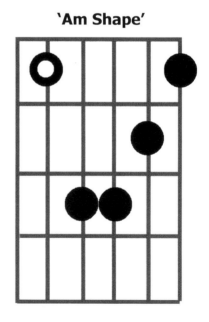

Our 'E shapes' work in exactly the same way using E Major and E minor shaped open chords barred with the 1st finger.

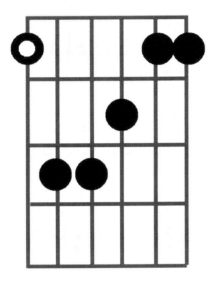

Our E Major chord shape barred with 1st finger.

This should feel more or less familiar because it's the same fingering as the 'A minor' shape that you've been doing for the B minor chord, everything is just up one string.

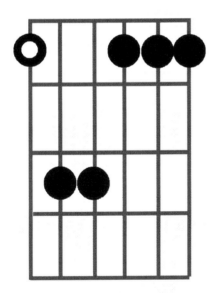

Our E minor chord shape barred with 1st finger.

Big barre on this one. That 1st finger has to work quite hard to hold down all 4 of those strings!

You'll notice I've added a white dot to these diagrams. This shows you root note of the chord. Wherever you move this note to will be the name of the chord. So if we consider these current positions at the 1st fret we have a B♭ Major and B♭ minor for our 'A shapes' and F Major and F minor for our 'E shapes'. But in order to do this thoroughly we need a reasonable understanding of the note names on our fretboard.... Guess whats coming next!...

NAME THAT NOTE!

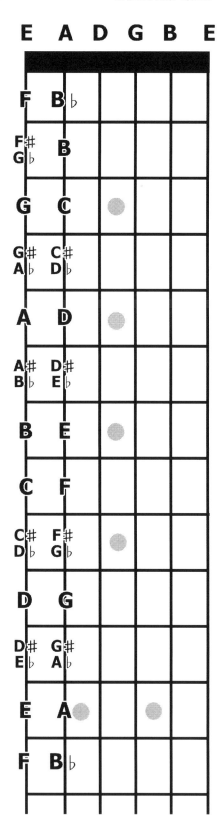

Here are the names of the 5th and 6th string notes on your fretboard.

The first thing to do is ignore any **enharmonic** notes. That is notes that have two names e.g F# and G♭ is one note with two names.

For now lets just play up our 6th string from E to E. As you do, play an 'E shape' Major chord on each note.

So E Major will be an open E chord. F Major is 1st fret using an 'E shape' barre chord. Move that same shape to the 3rd fret gives us G, 5th fret is A, 7th fret is a B, 8th is a C, 10th is D and 12th completes our octave with E.

You need to familiarise yourself with those notes, by doing that same exercise with the 'E shape' minor chords too.

And then move to the A string and do the same with your 'A shape' Major and minor bar chords.

The notes to pay particular attention to are the E to F and the B to C as you'll notice these are next to each other, where others have a fret between them. Under 'normal' circumstances there is no B# or C♭, or E# or F♭.

The best thing to do to get familiar with these is to play some of your favourite progressions using barre chords instead of open chords and get used to changing positions. It may seem like a backwards step at first because it's going to slow you down with progressions that you could otherwise play more easily, but get stuck in because we need these skills as we progress.

POWER CHORDS

To make things a little easier for a moment lets look at an alternative way to play these chords. Power chords!

Power chords are unlike 'normal' chords because the only contain two notes rather than the three (Root, 3rd, 5th) that we've been using up until now. Power chords only have a Root note and a 5th. In fact you will frequently see them referred to at '5' chords i.e A5, F5 etc. Because they have no 3rd interval we don't get strictly Major or minor power chords, they kind of have no flavour, consider them Vanilla. However, they do have a punch and are useful when you don't want too much melodic information in your chords.

Lets play some:

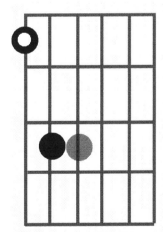 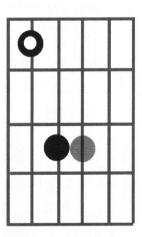

As you can see, regardless of which string we play them from the shape is the same. The first finger is the root and the 5th interval is on the string underneath, you could play this note with 3rd finger. The shaded note is an optional note - it's actually another Root note - including this can make the chord sound a bit beefier but is technically optional.

Hopefully you can see that these power chords are just the top three notes of any of your regular barre chords.

A I V vi IV progression in power chords:

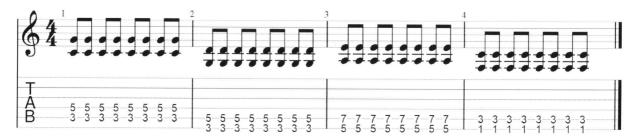

A riff idea using power chords:

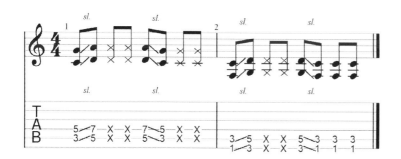

Throw in the chukkas for some punk attitude!

Some 'must know' power chord riffs worth looking at are:

Iron Man by Black Sabbath

Smells like Teen Spirit by Nirvana

Eye of the Tiger by Survivor

Song 2 by Blur

Seven Nation Army by White Stripes

Almost all Metal, rock and punk songs use power chord instead of 'real' chords. From Green Day to Metallica, you won't need to look far to find them.

Rock n Roll Rhythm

There is an old rock and roll rhythm technique that uses the power chord idea but adds a note, and then takes it away again. A good example is **Keep your Hands to Yourself** by **the Georgia Satellites** but the same riff can be found in lots of rock n roll and country rock songs.

Lets look at this idea in open position, as when played as a full power chord things can get stretchy. Lets play an open A power chord:

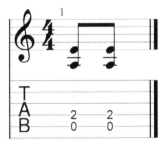

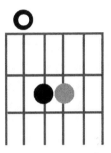

Here we're playing the open A (the root) and the 5th interval, the E, on the 4th string. As you can see from the chord diagram this is still our regular power chord shape.

The next bit is to add the 6th interval to it:

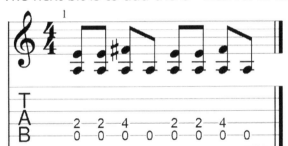

Use your 3rd finger to play the 4th fret (6th interval). How many beats you play this for will vary from song to song. It's commonly 2 beats of each chord, but you can get all sorts of variations.

Being a I IV V progression you would move the whole thing to the open D string for the D chord and down to the open E for the E chord.

Another variant is to also add in the 7th interval:

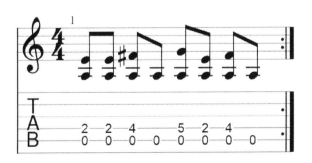

This is very common to a lot of blues tunes too, sounds great with a shuffled rhythm.

If you want to play it with non open string power chords then it's just a matter of holding the power chords as normal and extending your 4th finger to hit the 6th and 7th intervals - quite a stretch, sure, but worth the pain!

COMMON ALTERATIONS

The next step on our chord quest is to look at what we call alterations. This can become quite a complex topic so we're just going to focus on the most common alterations.

They are the sus4 and sus2. The 'sus' stand for suspended, and the 2 or 4 indicates the **interval** that we're using. For all of these examples we've replaced the 3rd for either the 2nd or 4th interval. More on intervals later but for now lets learn some more chords.

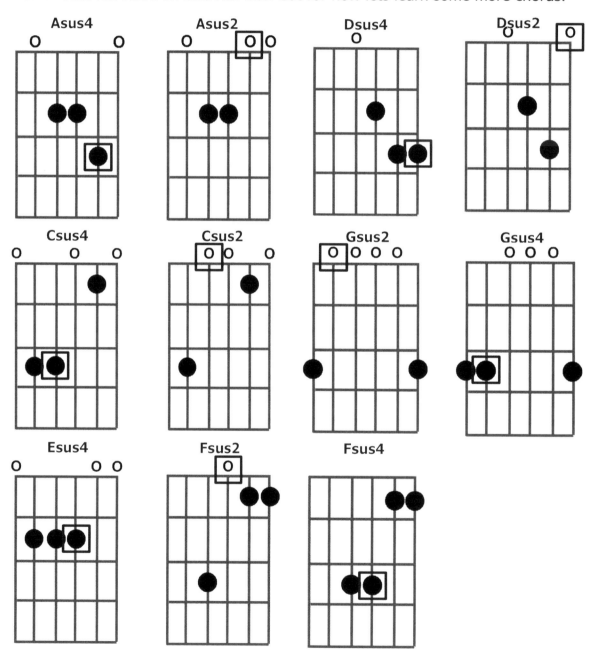

As you can see I've ☐ the 4th or 2nd so you can can see which notes are the sus notes. You should also compare these 4th's and 2nd's to the 3rd in your standard chords to make sure you understand where the alteration is.

Check out the acoustic version of Summer of 69 by Bryan Adam to hear a perfect example of both sus2 and sus4 chords.

Now, I'm personally not a big fan of Gsus (no religious pun intended) It sounds a little bottom heavy for my liking, and there are better options for playing this - like the movable F position. But you might like it - it might be just the chord you're looking for and may even save your chord progression - because, you know... Gsus saves... I'll get my coat...

Usage

So what's the point of these? and how do we use them outside of Gsus puns?

I'm glad you asked.

We can basically use them in place of your usual Major or minor chords. For instance you can use the Asus2 instead of a standard A chord. Because it loses the 3rd it no longer sounds as 'happy' as the A but retains the openness of the open chord.

| Asus2 / / / | C / / / :||

Sounds cool.

As we saw in the Bryan Adam's example people use them frequently to add movement to the chords specifically the 4th really likes to resolve to the 3rd. The Who's Pinball Wizard which starts on a Bsus4 chord resolve to the straight B chord. You can tell straight away that the sus4 want to resolve back to the 3rd.

The 2nd also want to resolve to the 3rd but less so, listen to the opening C chord of the Little Angels 'Don't Pray for Me' to hear Csus2 to C. Beautiful.

Another obvious lick is the opening to Crazy little thing called love by Queen. D to Dsus4 and back again. Very simple, very effective.

The Cadd9 Chord

Cadd9

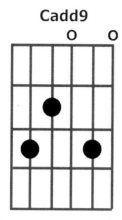

Cadd9 is such a common chord it really needs it's own page. You will frequently see this chord in place of the standard C chord. It's a cool sounding chord, but even cooler when you see how it's commonly used.

You play it exactly the same way you'd play an open G chord - as you can see it's the same shape, only on 5th an 2nd strings instead of 6th and 1st

This chord frequently finds itself between the G and D chords. Good Riddance by Green Day perfectly demonstrates this.

The great thing about this chord is it holds on to the D note. Because of this you may want to grow your G chord to include this note too:

G

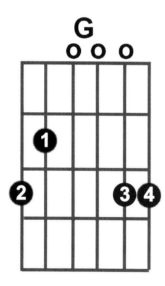

Playing it this way enables you to hang onto that D note with your 3rd finger throughout all the chords of the whole progression. Having a constant note in all the chords really helps them flow together smoothly.

Sweet Home Alabama also uses the Cadd9 for it's opening riff instead of a regular C.

As I said, there are so many examples of the Cadd9 that I'm sure it won't be long before you find songs yourself containing this idea. Look back at songs you previously did with the C chord - could you change it out for a Cadd9?

SCALES AND WAILS

PENTATONIC SCALES

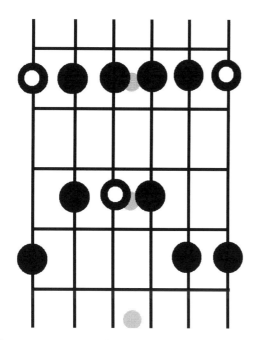

Welcome to every guitar players favourite scale - the Pentatonic scale.

Pentatonic scales are so called because they have only 5 notes - (Penta=5 and tonic=tones) instead of the 7 of our regular scales.

We're going to play this scale from the 5th fret which makes our root note an...

A!

Yes, well done, you have been paying attention!

If we count up the scale 5 notes from the root the next note is also an A, our next root.

Here it is in tab:

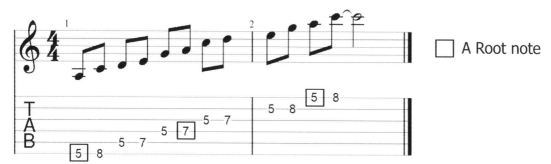

☐ A Root note

This scale is an **A minor pentatonic**. We start with this one because it's the most useful when improvising, as we'll soon discover. But it could be any minor Pentatonic scale, we name it by whatever the root note is on. Move that root to the 8th fret, it's a C minor pentatonic, move it to the 3rd fret and its a G minor pentatonic.

The minor pentatonic is constructed by using the 1 ♭3 4 5 ♭7 intervals. This is not information you need to particularly know, suffice to say that we know the ♭3 is what distinguishes a minor from a Major chord, well the same applies with scales. We also have a ♭7 in this one which we'll come to appreciate later.

Here's a nice little sequence to help you get used to the scale:

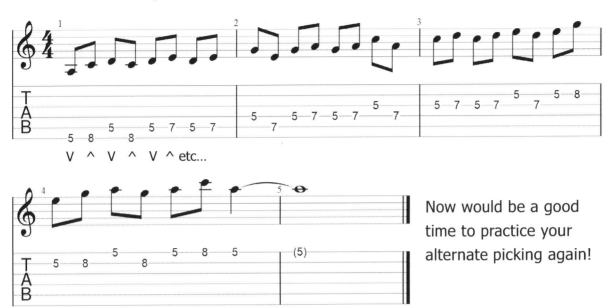

V ^ V ^ V ^ etc...

Now would be a good time to practice your alternate picking again!

The Chord connection

When looking at scales it's good to understand how they connect with chords - for now just trust me, it's a big deal!

So for this minor pentatonic scale I want you to be aware that there is a minor bar chord hiding within it:

'E shape' minor bar chord

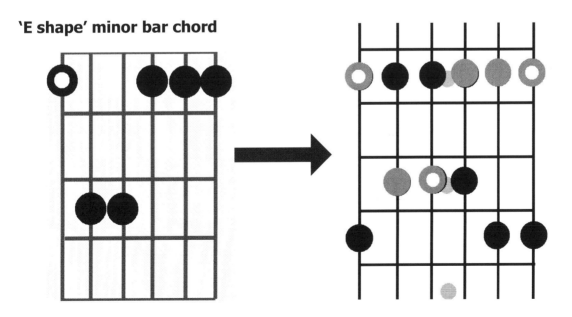

It's not what you play...

...It's how you play it! Lets learn some licks and techniques to give you some more ideas of stuff to play with that pentatonic scale and to generally spice up your playing a bit.

Bending

Bending is playing a note then pushing the string up until it sounds like a new note. Most of the time we want that new note to be a part of the scale too, so it will usually be the same as the note one or two frets away. This will be denoted in the tab by 'Full' or 'Half' - 'Full' being the fret two notes away as in the examples below, but sometimes you may get a 'half' which would indicate only one fret away.

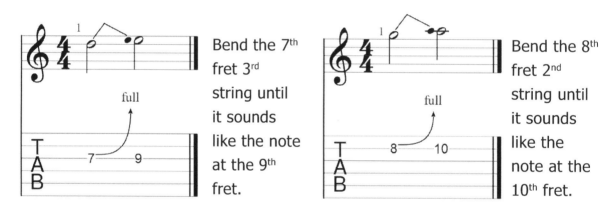

Bend the 7th fret 3rd string until it sounds like the note at the 9th fret.

Bend the 8th fret 2nd string until it sounds like the note at the 10th fret.

Notice that the note you are bending to is also a note of your pentatonic scale. So by bending to scale tones you can be sure you are staying in key.

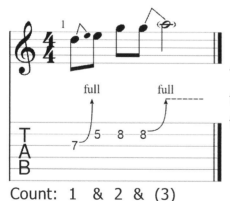

Try this phrase. The '7' bend should sound like the 9th fret and the '8' bend should sound like the 10th fret.

Count: 1 & 2 & (3)

This one is slightly different. We're going to bend the 7th fret (to sound like the 9th fret) and release the bend back to the 7th fret before moving on to finish the notes. Watch the timing, the bend is on the '1' beat and the release on the '&', the next two notes are on the '2' and 2'&' beats, this note then rings out for the '3' and '4' beats.

Count: 1(&) 2 & (3 4)

Sliding

Sliding is the technique of playing into a note from somewhere else. You could play a note on the 5th fret and slide your finger from there to the 7th fret (example 1.). Or play the 7th and slide to the 5th (example 2.). The point here is to only pick the string once. You pick the 5th fret, slide to 7th fret. If your slide is strong enough you won't need to re-pick the string - unless you want to for effect.

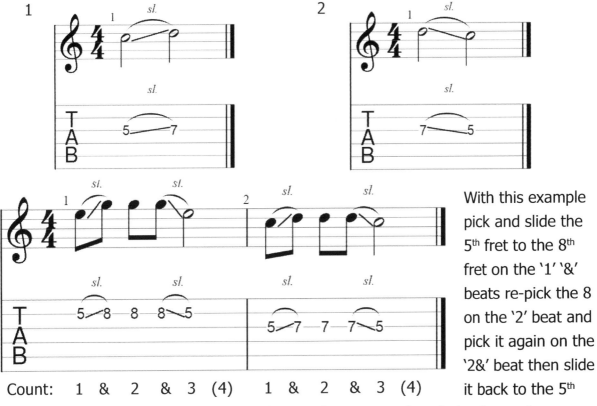

Count: 1 & 2 & 3 (4)   1 & 2 & 3 (4)

With this example pick and slide the 5th fret to the 8th fret on the '1' '&' beats re-pick the 8 on the '2' beat and pick it again on the '2&' beat then slide it back to the 5th fret letting it ring out for the '3' and '4' beats. Then repeat the whole phrase down one string between 5 and 7.

Hammering on and Pulling off

To **hammer on** a note is the concept of playing a note without picking it first - a bit like you did with the slide - you picked a note and then, without re-picking it, slid it to the next note. Hammer-on's are exactly the same but we don't slide we hammer!

Play the 5th fret with 1st finger and without re-picking the string 'hammer on' your 3rd finger to the 7th fret. The trick here is to get the string ringing well with the initial pick and also to get good contact when you 'hammer on'.

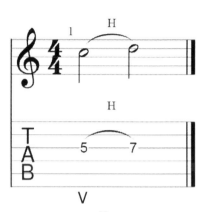

For a good hammer-on workout try playing the scale by only using hammer-on's therefore only picking each string once.

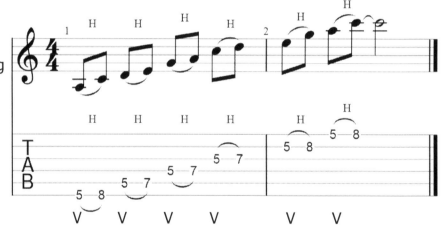

Pull offs

Put both your 1st and 3rd fingers on frets 5 and 7. Pick the 7 and swiftly remove ('pull off') your finger leaving the finger on 5. The 5 should ring out. You can accentuate this a little by pulling-off in a slightly downward motion to give the string a slight 'flick' as you go.

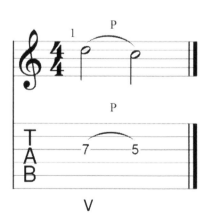

Just like with the hammer-on's also try the scale exercise with all pull-offs. Start at the high end and work low.

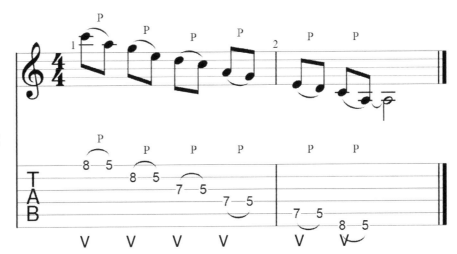

Here's a lick exercise to try combining hammer-on's and pull-off's.

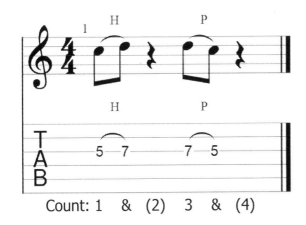

Count: 1 & (2) 3 & (4)

...and a much bigger cooler sounding one:

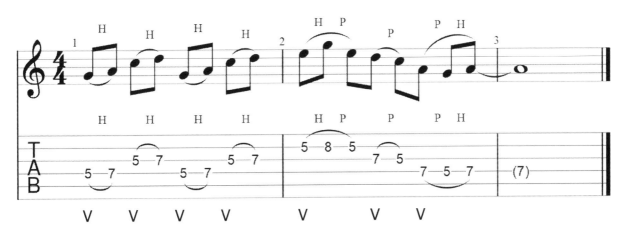

And try combining the hammer-on and pull-off scale exercises too!

LICKS!

Licks are cool little musical phrases we keep in our arsenal of 'things to play' - something that you need to build up so you don't run out of ideas when improvising.

Be warned though. When picking out licks from songs, some will rarely work outside of the song they're in. I frequently get people asking for a specific lick from a song because it sounds so awesome. However, it then frequently becomes apparent that the lick sounds good because of the context of the chords in the song. Once removed, it loses the thing that made your hairs stand up in the first place. So, what I've decided to do here is to only show mechanical licks. Things you can play in a scale but have little musical validity! I say that because you need to be aware that these are ideas that will help you own your scale position and exercise your fingers. They are good ideas that can be turned in to great music but that last bit is up to you! We'll address this as we go, but for now lets learn some licks!

Here you'll notice lots of repeating ideas. The idea being if you can play a phrase on one string or a pair of strings (ex 1.) then you play it on the next pair of strings as well, and maybe the next two too (ex 2.). This is a great idea for getting the most out of your licks, so always be moving them.

I've also tabbed them as eighth beat licks but they can be sped up to whatever speed you deem reasonable. As they get faster you will also want to incorporate hammer-on's and pull-off for notes on the same string. Look out for these as I've not tabbed hammer-on's and pull-offs given that you can play them anyway you like. Sometimes things sound good picked other times hammered and pulled. You decide what sounds good.

Ex 1.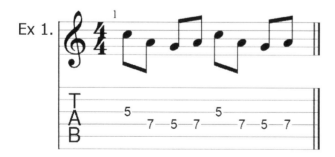

Ex 2.

Here's a repeating pattern of 4 notes descending one string at a time.

This is one of my favourites. Its a lick consisting of 4 notes, but because we ascend the same notes we end up with a 7 note phrase. When we then repeat the phrase it starts again on the 4 beat, and the next time on the 3 beat. This makes it much more unpredictable sounding. Make sure you count the beat slowly to get how this works:

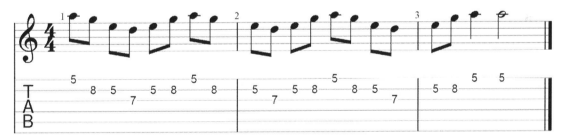

These next two are similar patterns that could be sped up to frightening speeds - if that's your thing!

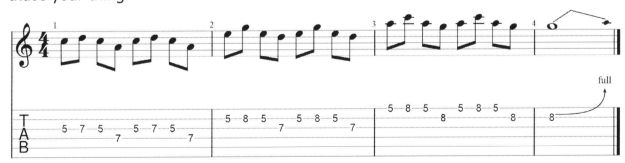

This one is the slightly trickier of the two watch the string changes.

This one is a combination of the last two.

Here's a cheesy rock 'n' roll inspired lick. Definitely one of those 'have to know it' licks. This has a triplet feel so count those threes, 1 2 3 1 2 3 etc...

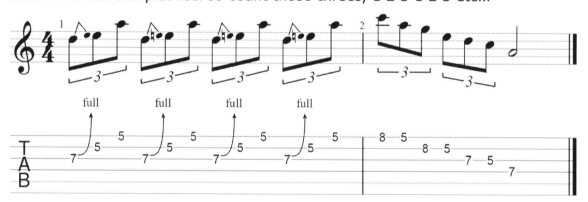

Cheesy rock lick number 2! Watch the timing we have a bend on 1 and then a quick triplet '1 2 3'.

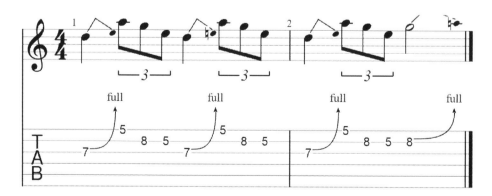

IMPROVISING

THE BLUES

Yep, guitar players do love to bang on about the blues and I appreciate if it's not your first choice of music then it's hard to get excited about. But here's the thing - Blues music not only forms the foundation of loads of pop and rock music but it also somewhat contradicts some concepts of traditional music theory, and as guitarist we tend to like stuff that breaks the rules.

Play that funky music...

So let's play something. First of all you'll need a backing track. We're doing some Blues so we'll use a 12 bar I IV V progression in A, so A, D and E. But here's the first thing I want you to be aware of - A, D and E is an A **Major** I IV V progression and we're going to play an A **minor** pentatonic scale over it! This is what distinguishes a 'blues' progression from a strict **diatonic** (of a specific key) progression. Playing minor pentatonics over Major chords has a certain flavour that we call 'bluesy'.

So record yourself play a I IV V in A or find a backing track somewhere and 'noodle' the minor pentatonic scale over the top of it.

The first thing you'll want to do is run up and down the scale and get used to the sound over the chord progression, particularly listen and be aware of when the chords are going to change. You're going to want to anticipate those changes soon. Also don't forget to throw in some of those lick ideas we did previously, see if you can get them to fit or adjust them to suit.

Call and response

You'll also want to know where your root note is, in this case the A. You'll want to create licks that reinforce that root note. There is an improvisation idea called 'call and response' playing. This is where you'll create a phrase that sounds unfinished, and then finish it. In this case we'll use a phrase that lands on any note other than the Root. This is the 'call' part - because you didn't land on the Root, it'll sound unfinished, like you're pausing and adding some anticipation (**tension**) of what is coming next. You'll then 'respond' to that phrase by playing something that finishes on the Root which will then sound complete (**release**). Think of it like speaking or writing with commas (non Root notes) for pauses, and finish will full stops (Root notes) to highlight the end. This is the concept of **tension and release** that keeps us interested in a piece of music.

Play the Chord Changes

Once you're happy with the scale and have been experimenting a while with phrases you might want to look more closely at the chord changes.

What you'll notice when you listen to a lot of licks is that they have a tendency to highlight the chord tones of the chord they're being played over. This sounds complicated... and in all honesty... yeah, it's a bit hard! But, this is why, when you learn your favourite lick from your favourite song, and when improvising you throw it out there, for some reason it now sounds a bit rubbish. It's because most great licks emphasise the chords they are played over. A good example is the first lick in the solo to Stairway to Heaven, it's great, but it ends on an F note... that F note doesn't always translate if you play it over a different A minor chord progression, so if you steal that lick you'll probably have to change the end to fit your progression.

However, we're not playing Stairway, but we need to know how to navigate our chord changes just the same.

In our 12 bar progression we have three chord changes. The A, the D and the E. It's a good exercise to highlight these tones as the chords change. So, for the first lot of A bars, you can use the A root and use your call and response technique so things don't sound too stale. When you anticipate the D chord hit a D note or play a phrase that finishes on the D note. It's still so satisfying to hit a root note on a chord change, it just sounds so right and like you meant it... Because we did, right!

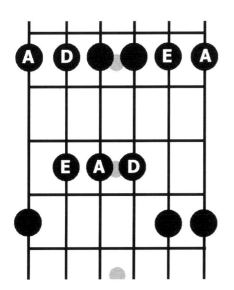

And then the same on the E chord change. Play a phrase and end on the chord change with an E note... sounds so cool!

But it's not the only thing that works, so whilst it really helps you nail those changes it's not a hard and fast rule. You should also consider phrases that just *include* the Root notes rather than land on them, this can be just as effective for outlining the changes as landing directly on the root. Experiment. This is why we start with the blues - it's harmonically so loose we can try out lots of ideas!

Ignore the Chord Changes!

A great example of not playing the changes is to play a phrase that works over each change. For instance, try this one:

Play this phrase continuously over the whole 12 bar progression regardless of changes. You'll notice that it 'fits' every chord, but also changes the flavour very slightly as each chord changes.

Or remember this idea:

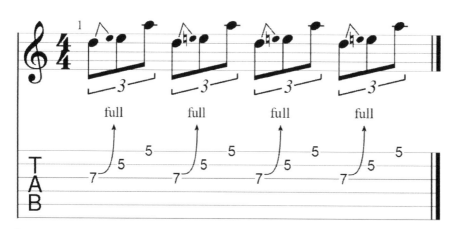

As with the first one, just play it continuously over the whole progression - it's a finger workout mind you! But, once again, you'll see that it works regardless of

the chord it's played over.

Cool huh! You can find lots of these ideas with a bit of experimenting so check them out!

However, do note that the more complicated your chord progression gets the more these ideas will start to fail, but for simple ideas we can have simple solutions!

Obviously, you'd be a little odd if you played one repeating idea over an entire progression, like the guitarist equivalent of a needle stuck in vinyl so best to just engage in the repeating licks technique sparingly!

RELATIVELY SPEAKING

Remember when we talked about all chords having a **relative** minor - C Major had a **relative** A minor. Well, we can turn that around too. We've just done an **A minor pentatonic scale**, well, we can also see this as a **C Major pentatonic scale**. *Mind blown*!

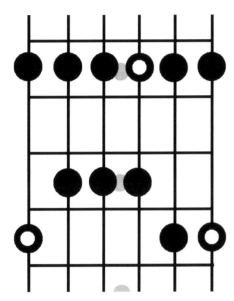

So, you should recognise this 'shape' from a few pages ago as an A minor pentatonic scale. Except I've changed the root notes from an A to a…. I'll wait… 8th fret, 6th string is a….

…??

C !

Now this can get confusing. As you know, if you play these notes from the A note (5th fret) you get an A minor scale. But if you play them from the 8th fret C, you get a **C Major pentatonic scale**.

Check it out, play this:

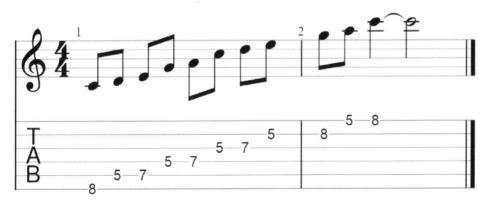

Did if sound like a happier scale than when you started from A?

Ok, let's play with it. For comparisons sake we'll use the same backing track as we just did - the 12 bar in A - but this time we want it to sound happier. So we're going to play the **A Major pentatonic** scale over it instead of the A minor pentatonic scale. To do this we need to put our root note on the A. We know that's the 5th fret on our 6th string but remember that in the Major pentatonic the root is on our 4th finger. In current position we're in C Major so we need to move the scale down 3 frets so instead of the root being a C at the 8th fret it becomes an A at the 5th fret.

So we're actually going to play this scale between the 2nd and 5th frets.

Or, if this was a minor pentatonic scale, it would be a....?

F# minor pentatonic!

Just like A minor and C Major share the same notes, so do A Major and F# minor. The two scales are the same notes it just depends from which root note you're thinking. They are **Relative Scales.**

Anyway, moving on...

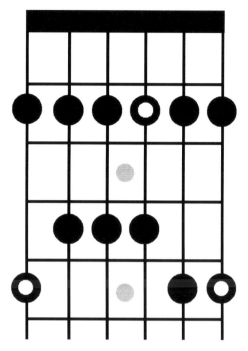

Now, just like you did before play over the 12 bar progression - A D E. If you've just come from playing the minor scale you may need to acclimatise your ears to the new sound. At first it could sound 'wrong' to you, it's not, it's just different!

So do everything you did before - Play up and down the scale for a bit to get used to the sound and then experiment with those same licks we had before. What you do need to be aware of it that our Roots have changed position.

Before, when playing in A minor, you probably got used to this note:

The Root note A on the 4th string is frequently our 'safe' note when playing A minor blues.

However, in A Major, that note is now on the **2nd fret 3rd string**. So you'll need to adjust your licks around that note instead.

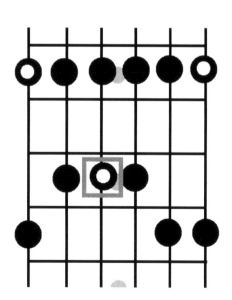

Play the Chord Changes

A cool thing when playing the Major scale over Major chords is that you can move the scale with the chord, so if you're playing over the A chord, you play the A Major pentatonic.

This is a good way to visualise your 'A shape chord' in your Major pentatonic scale.

So wherever you play an **'A Shape' Major chord** you can play this scale over it.

This Major pentatonic over 'A shape' chord is a common Keef Richards/Rolling Stones or even Jimi Hendrix style trick - you'll find all those great notes are connected to that A shape. It's common for people to play the 'A shape' with just the first finger and then add or improvise the scale notes to the chord.

If you want to visualise it with the 5th string root it looks like diag.1 :-

Over our D chord you'd play the pentatonic shape between 7th and 10th fret - the A shape being on 7th fret. Likewise with the E chord, you'd use these same position but move everything up 2 frets so the root is on E.

You can also visualise a 'G chord shape' from the 6th string root if you really want to blow your mind! However, at the moment, this is less useful because we rarely use G shape chords as movable chord ideas.

A Major Chord

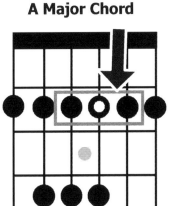

Diag.1.

D Major Chord

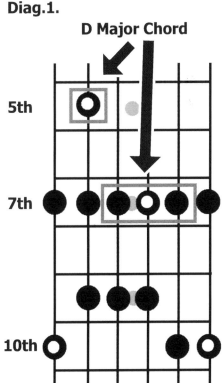

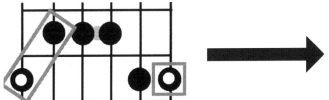

Mixing them up

The next trick in the book of blues players is not sticking to one scale. As we've seen both the minor pentatonic and the Major pentatonic work over a I IV V progression. But what you can also do is to use both in the same progression. The most popular way to do this is to play the Major pentatonic on the I chord - so A in our example - and the A minor pentatonic on the IV and V chords - D and E in our example.

You can hear recorded examples of this in the solo's to the song Crossroads by Eric Clapton or The Jack by ACDC, where both solos open with Major phrases and then change to minor pentatonics.

Try it. Remember always be playing this stuff yourself. Don't just take my word for it!

So to clarify

Over our A D E 12 bar progression you can play:

The A minor pentatonic over every chord.

A Major pentatonic over every chord.

A D & E Major pentatonic over their named chord.

A Major pentatonic on the A chord and A minor pentatonic on the D and E chords.

There, that should keep you busy for a bit!

How to Count Like Dracula

URGHHH DOTS?!

So what happened to 'no need to read notes'?!

Well, here we're reading rhythms and not strictly 'dots' but most importantly, rhythms are everything!

Whether you are strumming or wailing solos your timing is the most important aspect of your playing. Imagine any classic riff you like, whether its 'Smoke on the Water', 'Seven Nation Army' or 'Whole Lotta Love', they all have rhythm, and if you took that rhythm away the notes would have no meaning. If I wrote this paragraph without full stops, spaces, or comma's, the line between a meaningful text and a jumble of letters would soon become blurred. Rhythm in music is our spaces, comma's and full stops.

You have to be aware that learning rhythm is not just so you can read it in dots, it's so you have a methodically way to break down what you hear and understand it. This allows you to experience a wider range of rhythmic ideas thus giving you options to make better rhythmic choices when you play.

What I would recommend is for you to become more aware of exactly what's going on in the rhythms you hear when you're listening to music. Tapping your foot is the first part of this. Being able to tell where a beat is in relation to your foot tap is the first part of 'feeling' rhythm. Your foot will hit the 1 beat, but the note your listening to came after the 1 - so how far after the 1 did it come? It's answering these kinds of questions that will enable you to start become more aware of how these beats are broken down.

You then need to apply this to your phrasing when you're playing. Consider rhythmic divisions to be options you have when phrasing, it really can make all the difference to play a note a sixteenth away from where it was expected! And remember that the note would've been the same wherever you played it, so it's effect on the listener is all ...

....

....

.....

...timing!

DIVIDE AND CONQUER!

Up until now we've mainly focused on dividing our bars into quarter notes - 4 beats to a bar, eighth notes - 8 beats to a bar, with a few triplet 'feels' thrown in, whether as a ¾ time signature count or as quarter note triplets - 12 notes to a bar.

Before we move on lets do some revision:

Whole notes - 1 note to a bar

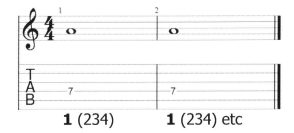

Half notes - 2 notes to a bar

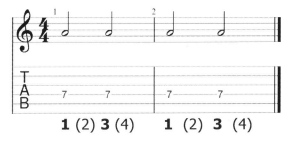

Quarter notes - 4 beats per bar

Combination Practice Piece

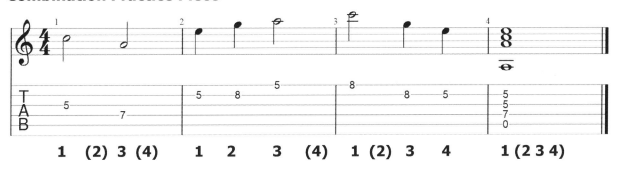

Eighth notes - 8 notes per bar

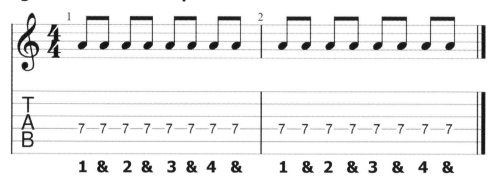

Quarter note triplets - 3 notes per beat

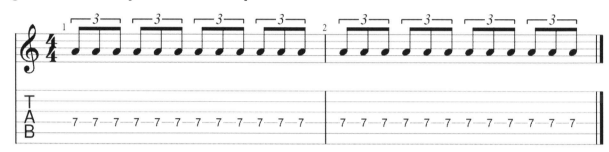

Sixteenth notes - 4 notes per quarter note - each quarter note is split into 4 equal notes and counted 1 e & a

Combination Practice Piece

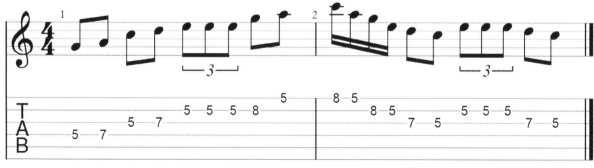

Next we have some combinations of notes. This one is an eighth note followed by two sixteenths. So we count the '1 &' as we would with a regular eighth beats but we add the 'a' as the last beat is a sixteenth. Or you could see it that it's a sixteenth with the 'e' missed out...

1(e)& a 2(e)& a 3(e)& a 4(e)& a ...etc

This is the opposite of the above one. We have the first bit of a sixteenth but with an eighth at the end. So we count the 1 e & but that last & is an eighth so we pause on that note for the remainder of the beat - so no 'a'.

1 e &(a) 2 e &(a) 3 e &(a) 4 e &(a) etc...

Combination Practice Piece

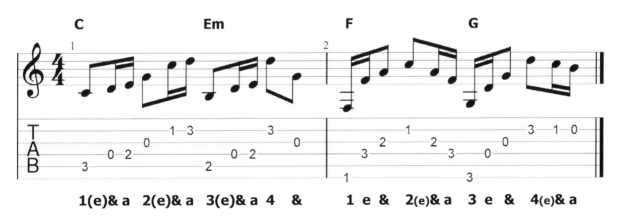

1(e)& a 2(e)& a 3(e)& a 4 &   1 e &   2(e)& a   3 e &   4(e)& a

This is much harder because I've based the melody around chord shapes. Hold the chord shape as directed when possible and then add the other notes.

Dotted Notes

If there is a small dot behind a note it means that note is worth **half its time again.** Look I didn't make this stuff up, I just have to pass the information on!

So with our note that's worth 2 beats, it's now worth 3 beats.

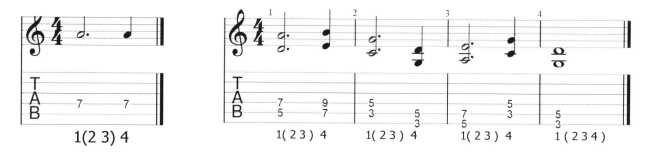

Our quarter note that was worth 1 beat is now worth 1 and a half - so 1 beat and one eighth note.

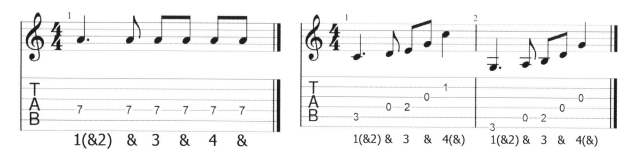

And an eighth note is now worth an extra sixteenth

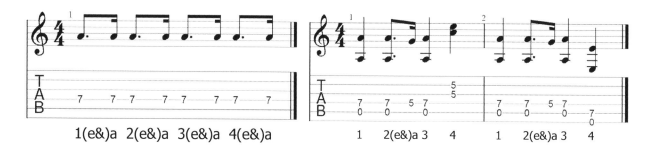

This last one is pretty awkward when you're new to it. But its a very groovy rhythm, once you get the feel for it, it can feel quite natural.

CONNECTING SCALES

MAJOR PENTATONIC SCALES

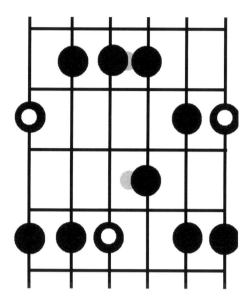

Here's a position 1 Major pentatonic scale. Before, when we experimented with the Major pentatonic, we viewed it from 1st position of the minor pentatonic scale. We'll see how these two scales connect in a bit, but first I want to show you why this is considered position 1 for the Major.

Just like it's minor counterpart, we can fit the E Major shape bar chord right into the scale:

'E Major' shape bar chord

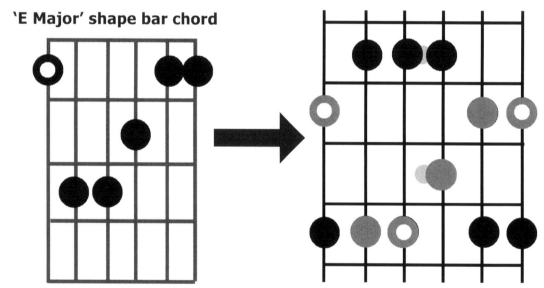

To get familiar with this shape I'd encourage you to play the chord and then play the scale to really reinforce the connection. Don't worry about using it for any improvisation yet, we'll do that shortly. Just get a feel for how the scale wraps around the chord.

We generally consider the lowest note Root on the on the 6th string as the Position 1 scale. There are 5 pentatonic positions in all. The minor pentatonic position 1 is the Major Position 5. But pfft, numbers eh… ! We'll clarify the numbers later…

Making the connection

So here's the diagram that's going to bring everything together. You can see that we have the minor pentatonic position connected to the Major pentatonic position.

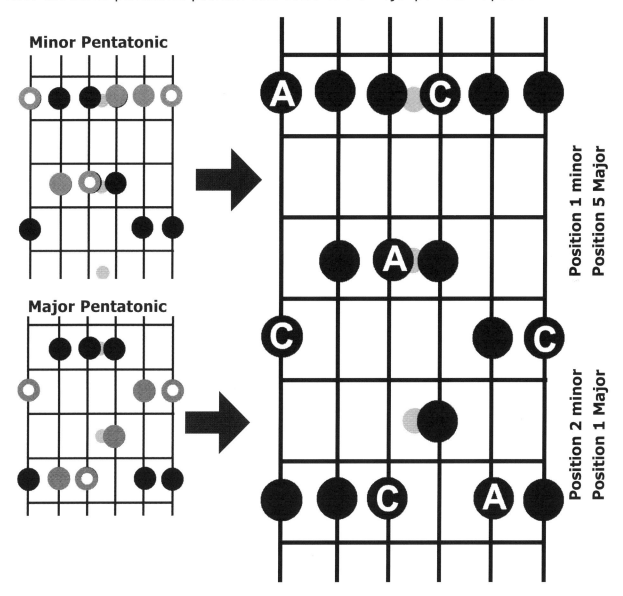

Remember, C Major and A minor share the same notes! They are **Relative scales.** So we can think of them as the same shapes - we can consider the shape above one shape and play in either A minor or C Major. However, when learning it's easier to consume this information if we break it into these smaller shapes first. It's also really helpful melodically if we can see the chord connections...

Chord Connections

Remember when I said I preferred the term 'movable chords' to 'Barre chords' well this is why. All those open position chords are really only **shapes**. They are all movable to an extent and depending on where you put the root note determines the chord name.

Here's one of the most useful tricks you'll ever have. Visualising chords in scales. We've seen the two big ones - the 'E shape' bar chords - one in A minor and one in C Major. Well, hidden below there is also a 'G Major open position' shape chord as well as an 'D minor open position' shape chord.

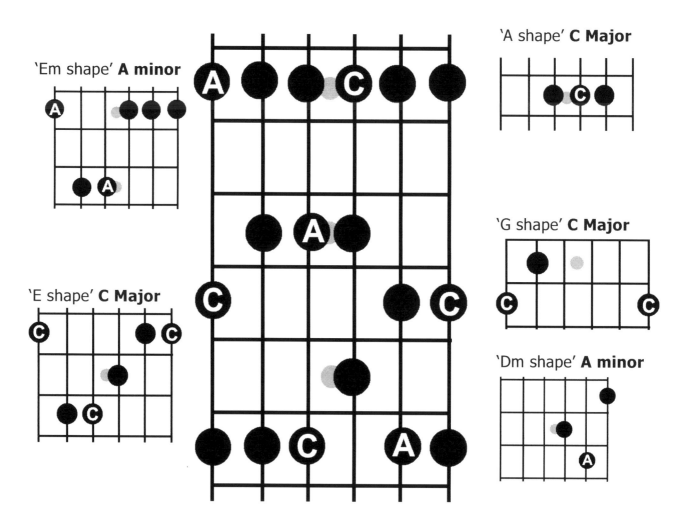

'Em shape' **A minor**

'A shape' **C Major**

'G shape' **C Major**

'E shape' **C Major**

'Dm shape' **A minor**

Remember: These hidden chords are '**shapes**'. The 'G chord **shape**' is actually a C chord because the root note in on a C - **it is a G in shape only**. Likewise the 'D minor **shape**' is actually an A minor chord because the root in an A.

98

ARGHHHH!
TOO MUCH INFORMATION!

Yes, this is where most students start to hit critical mass. It becomes a case of information vs useful information and a big 'what's the point' question mark appears over their head as if waiting for a quest.

So lets make sure we can make all of this information useful and the way we do that is with melodic context.

Remember when we were playing our A minor Blues improvisation and we had that safe 'A' note... you know, this one:

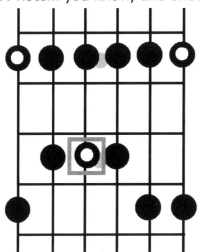

Well, that occurs because you ears can detect this note as a safe haven and you 'feel' it as 'the right note to play' especially when you finish a phrase - because it's a Root note. Well, lets expand this idea into the position we just looked at. Lets play an A minor pentatonic scale but flow from position 1 into our new position:

Watch the slide on the 3rd string. Use your 3rd finger to slide and the your 1st finger on the 2nd string 8th fret to keep good position.

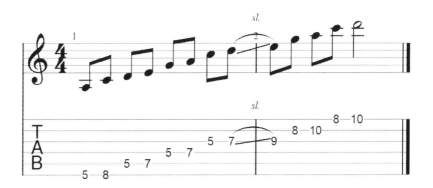

So we've gone from position 1 minor pentatonic into position 1 C Major pentatonic - only we don't want to think of it like that at all!... When in minor pentatonics will think of Major position 1 as minor position 2 - so we've moved from minor pos.1 to minor pos.2.

99

Now experiment with some improvising over the A Blues as you previously did and get used to this new pattern and meet me below when you're done.

Hey! How've you been? Got that little extension sorted?

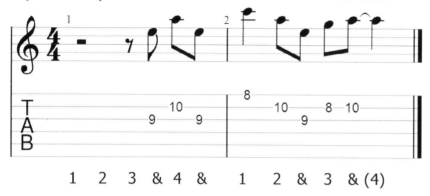

Right, look at this lick.

Watch the timing on this - it starts on the & of 3, so make sure you give yourself the correct count in.

1   2   3 & 4 &   1   2 & 3   & (4)

So, what makes this an effective lick? Let's look at this bit:

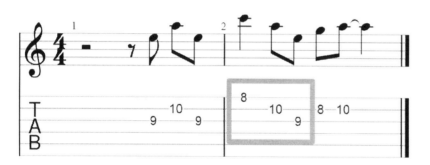
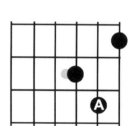

If you finger just these notes you'll see they form that D minor open position chord shape. Except as we saw previously it's now an A minor chord. So we've just outlined the notes of A minor in a lick. This makes it fit perfectly over an A minor chord or our 'key ambiguous' blues progression.

The lick also works here:

Because:

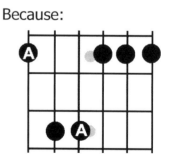

Outlining chords really is the key to melodic context. I said at the very beginning something about people taking licks out of songs and then wondering why they don't sound great anymore. This is that reason. Melodies and chords go together!

Try this lick over a C Major chord.

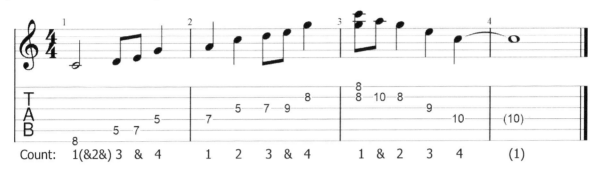

See if you can see how the chords connect with this one. To demonstrate I've added the notes under the tab so you can see how most of this lick is just the notes of a C Major chord - C E G.

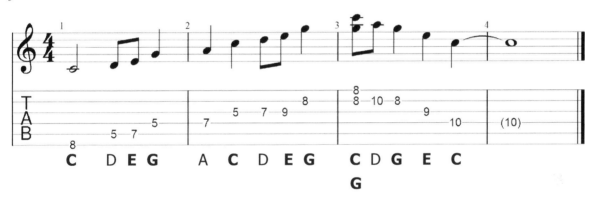

This is great information and a really useful guide to help with improvisation and just playing more musically in general. But how can we practice it more efficiently?...

ARPEGGIOS

WHAT'S AN ARPEGGIO?

An arpeggio is literally a broken chord. No really, it's a chord played a note at a time - broken into individual notes. In the previous chapter we used chord tones to create licks, and arpeggios are a great way to practice these chord shapes within scales to enable you to greatly visualise how things connect on your neck.

If you remember, chords consist of 3 notes; a root, the 3rd and the 5th. We're going to play these arpeggios in that interval order.

A minor arpeggio

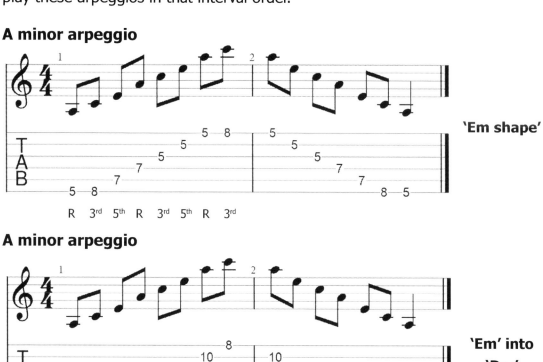

'Em shape'

R 3rd 5th R 3rd 5th R 3rd

A minor arpeggio

'Em' into 'Dm' shape

R 3rd 5th R 3rd 5th R 3rd

C Major arpeggio

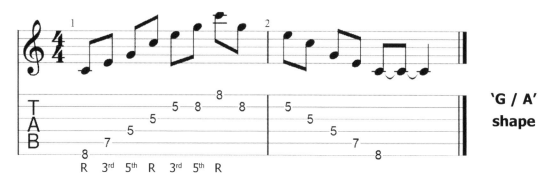

'G / A' shape

R 3rd 5th R 3rd 5th R

C Major arpeggio

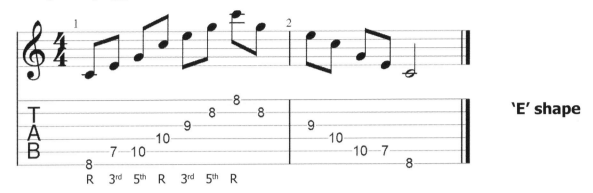

'E' shape

Remember these are to aid your visualisation of where your chord tones are. I wouldn't necessarily recommend playing them straight up and down when improvising, you'll want to be grabbing little melodic snippets from them instead. Like this:

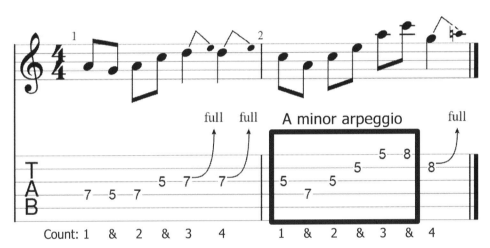

Ok, I need you to put your concentration trousers on for this next bit, it could get hairy...

So, recap, this one:

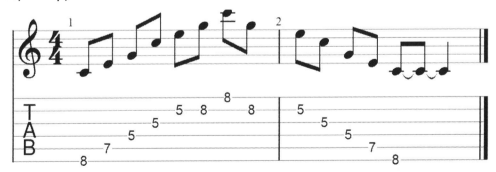

We did this over there on the previous page right... but now we're going to put the root note on a new string so it looks like...

...this:

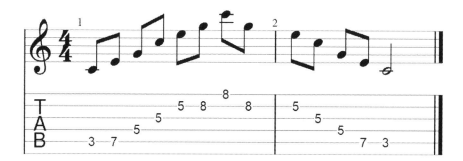

Remember this:

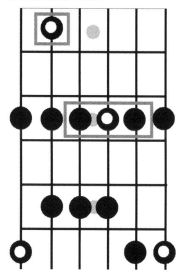

We looked briefly at this shape during the improvising section, so we know when faced with an 'A shape' chord we have two Roots to visualise it from - a 5th string Root and a 6th string Root.

I want to focus on the 5th string Root for this next bit.

We're going to extend the scale to include the C Major position 1 and view the whole thing from this 5th string root note.

Like this:

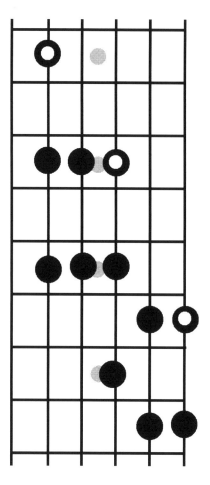

You could play this as a straight pentatonic like this:

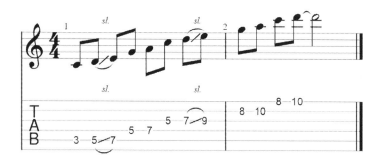

Or as just the arpeggio notes:

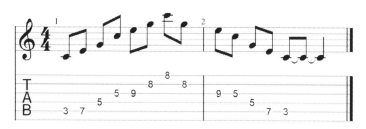

Whats the big idea?

So to wrap up I want to clarify that with all these exercises and arpeggios, I want you to be able to visualise the fret board like this:

C Major Pentatonic positions
with 'A shape' C chord and
'E shape' C chord

A minor Pentatonic positions
with 'Em shape' Am chord and
'Dm shape' Am chord

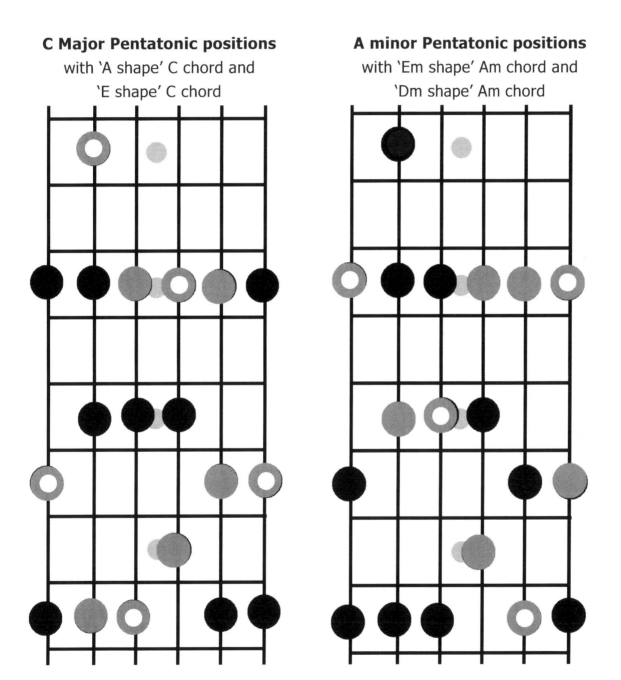

Rhythm Guitar

RHYTHM GUITAR ISN'T BORING....

Up until now when playing 'rhythm' guitar we've been strumming chords. That's fine. All good. Sometimes when it's your job to keep time and fill out the rhythm section all you want to be doing is strumming chords. However, there is a place where we can do more than just strum chords. If you listen to the likes of Stevie Ray Vaughan, Jimi Hendrix , John Mayer, John Frusciante... actually the list is once again endless... but these players rarely just play a straight chord. You'll frequently hear melody ideas played alongside the chord and this is what we're going to look at now.

The great thing is that you already have all the tools! Everything we do here you already know, it's just a good excuse to put into practice the chords and scales we've done up until now.

Firstly I want to clarify the point that all chords and scales are movable. If we play this chord:

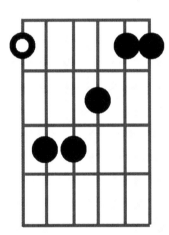

...then this scale fits it - **wherever we play it.**

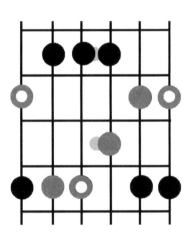

> **Scales can move with chords.**

Return of the vi IV I V

Lets use our vi IV I V chord progression to put some of this in practice and to get our creative juices flowing.

|Am | F | C | G |

Play it quite slowly, if you have a metronome go to somewhere around 70bpm, we want those bars to last quite a long time.

You should be aware that there are at least a couple of places you can play each chord but I'm going to give you a couple of examples before you get let loose.

We're going to use these chord positions:

Am at 5th fret   F at 8th fret   C at 8th fret   G at 3rd fret

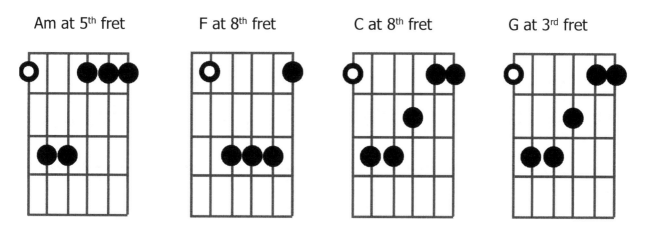

Do this for a bit and get used to the changes, use any strumming pattern you like for now but keep it slow.

Once you're used to it try phrasing around each chord in it's position then turn the page for an example.

Rhythm phrasing example

So whats going on here then?

Lets start by laying out the chords for each section...

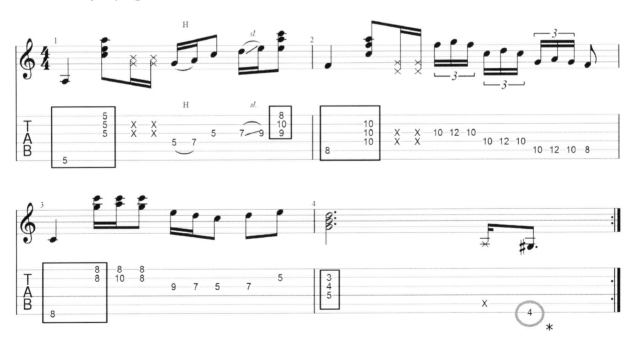

Hopefully you can see from this example that I've boxed in the chord shapes. As you can see you don't always have to play the whole chord. Breaking chords into smaller chunks often gives the music more life and space. Especially when playing with a band - you might not want to emphasise the low notes when that's your bass players job, or the high bits if your keyboard player has them covered, so always feel free to play just the bit of the chord you want to.

When breaking chords up like this you can hold down the whole chord and just pick the bits you want, or you can play the bits separately - we call these **chord fragments** - and they're very useful melodic devices.

Once we've outlined the chord we can then put a phrase or melodic idea around the chord using it's associated pentatonic scale, here's a reminder of the positions used in this example...

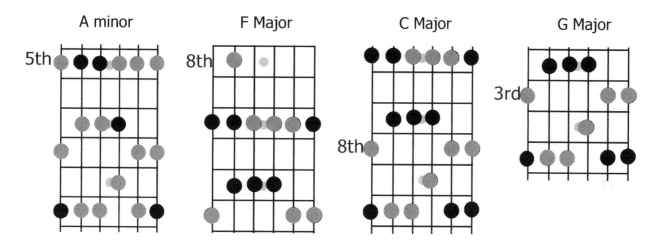

* The G♯ note circled in this example is not in the pentatonic scale or chord of G Major. It's use is to add tension to the repeat. It works because being a half step lower than A it makes us anticipate the A chord that comes on the next beat.

Lets do one more. New chord progression: I vi V IV in C .

| C | Am | G | F ||

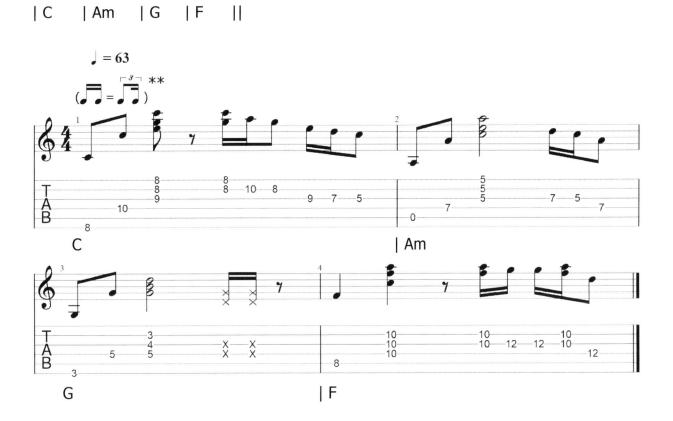

Lets examine this one.

Bar 1: C Major 'E shape' bar chord + Major position 1, 8th fret.
Bar 2: A minor 'Em shape' bar chord + Minor position 1, 5th fret.
Bar 3: G Major 'E shape' bar chord + Major position 1, 3rd Fret.
Bar 4: F Major 'A shape' bar chord + Major position 5, 8th Fret.

Remember to add your own fills and personality.

A nice alternative way to try this chord progression is to descend every chord on the 6th string. So play C Major at 8, the Am at 5, G at 3 and F at 1st fret, and see if you can play some fills in those positions.

** This indicates the type of groove added to the notes. However, for this example it is completely ignore-able!

PLAYING WITH INTERVALS

A NEW APPROACH

Right let's try a new approach. We've done scales and we've done chords, let try a chord scale!

Keeping in our now very familiar C Major scale. Let's ascend in the key of C our two A shape bar chords, Major and minor, starting on our 5th string root.

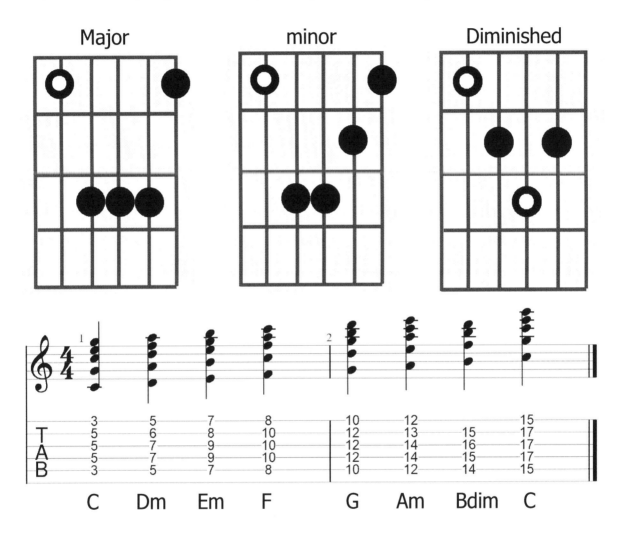

Remember the pattern?: M m m M M m d

Now, if you run up those chords you should hear that familiar Major scale sound but you'll hear it accompanied by all those nice chord harmony notes too. Like a choir of Angels!

And with E chords...

Same idea on your 6th string looks like this:

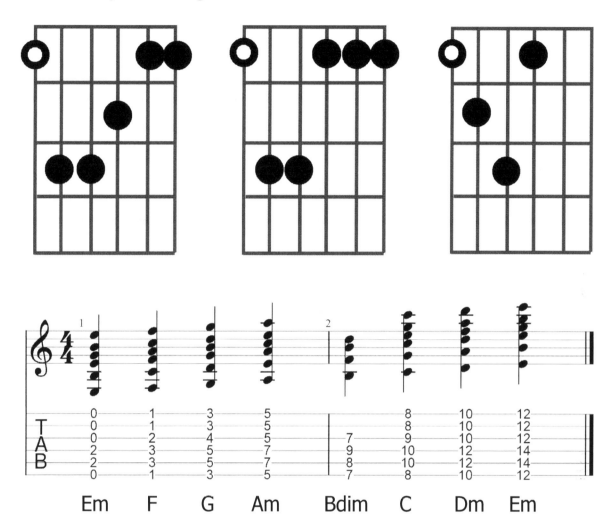

This won't sound as obvious because we're starting on Em instead of C so you lose that Major scale sound, but do it anyway yeah!

Octaves and Thirds

Next lets simplify them. Lets play just root notes.

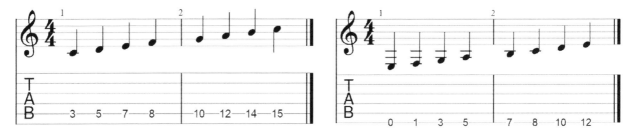

We know where the 5th and 6th string root notes are, lets now find the octave i.e the same note but eight notes higher. To do this we simply skip a string and a fret. Sometimes you'll see Octave written like '8ve' or '8va'.

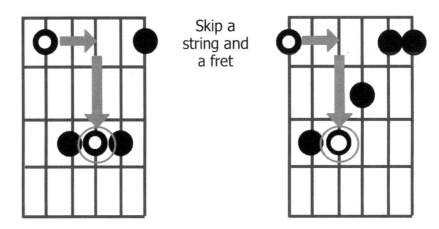

Skip a string and a fret

This is an Octave.
2 root notes an 'Octave' apart.

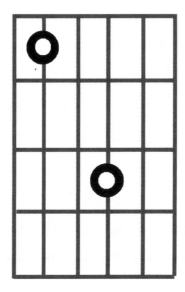

FRETBOARD NOTES

With knowing your 6th and 5th string notes we can combine the octave skip to discover the notes on the 4th and 3rd strings.

Look at the diagram to the right. This is all your fretboard notes.

Find a note on the 6th or 5th string and see how, if you skip a string and a fret, you reach the same note an octave higher.

You can now find any note on your 4th and 3rd strings using this method. This will help make it easier to memorise them.

Unfortunately the octave trick doesn't work for your last two strings because the 2nd string is tuned differently to the rest. What you have to do instead is to compensate by one fret. So to find the 2nd and 1st string octaves you skip 2 frets instead of 1.

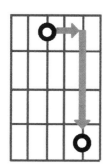 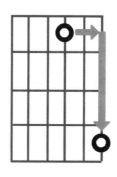

You can now use these two shapes to learn the notes of your entire fretboard!

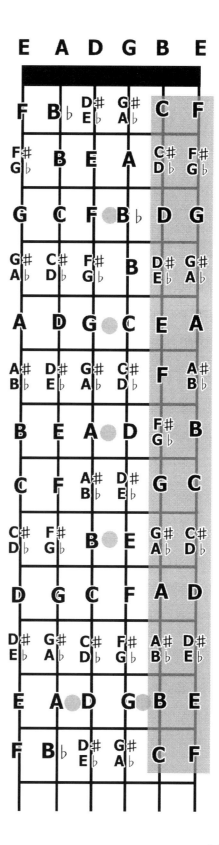

119

Anyway... where were we?!

Oh yes...

Octaves

Here's the C Major scale in octaves:

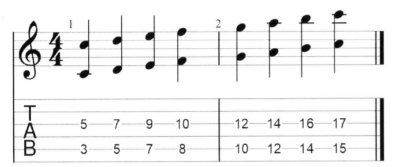

Octave are also useful device for playing melodies or chords. From the likes of Hendrix to Wes Montgomery to Steve Vai, Eric Johnson to Pat Metheny, everyone plays octaves:

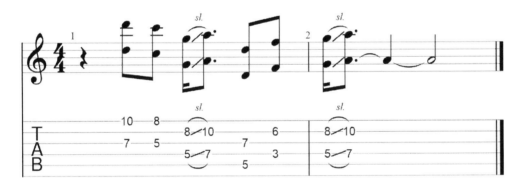

Octaves are really good at thickening up a melody line or creating a heavy riff between power chords:

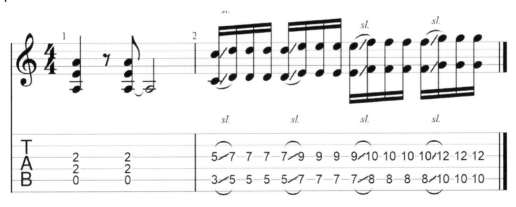

Thirds

Octaves don't really have a harmony as such, they're nice an' all, but let's add a harmony.

The third, as you know by now, is the note that determines whether we have a Major or a minor chord.

Try this:

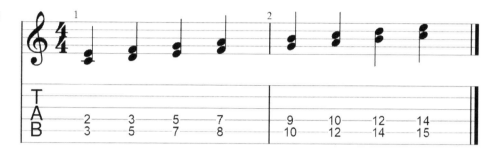

Sounds familiar right? It's our chord scale again, but instead of having the 3rd in the chord we've put it on the 4th string. So we have root on 5th and the third on the 4th string. To make it more visual, if you compare your open C chord to the first note here you'll see you've played the top two notes of that C chord, and then, as with movable chords, we've moved it up using our M m m M M m d sequence.

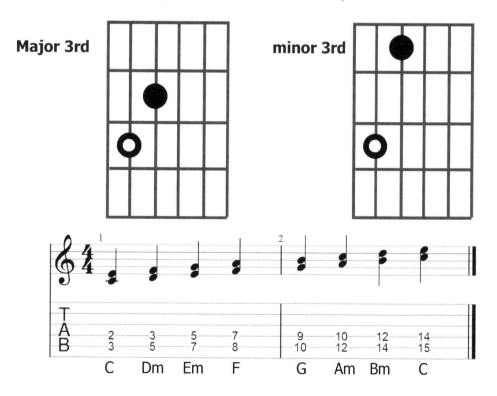

So to clarify, we have a Major interval to start, we then have the same idea on D but we flatten the third to give us the minor interval, that's why its a step away unlike the C interval.

Try this on your E root too, but do it as G Major so you can hear the Major scale as you go. You know the notes. Start on the 3rd fret with G, which you know is a Major third, then A on 5th, which you know is minor third. See if you can create the Major scale harmony by ear, or by knowledge. Answer below so no cheating!

Did you get it?

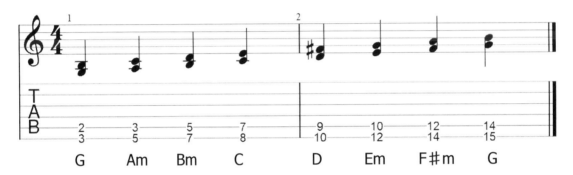

Tenths

For the next one we're going to move the third back to where it was in the chord. We frequently actually call this a 'tenth' rather than a 'third', even though its the same note, we frequently like to distinguish which octave a note is in, so a third would be the note in the first octave and the tenth would be a note in the second octave. We never go more than two octaves though, that would be getting silly.

So here's the Root and tenth going up the C Major scale:

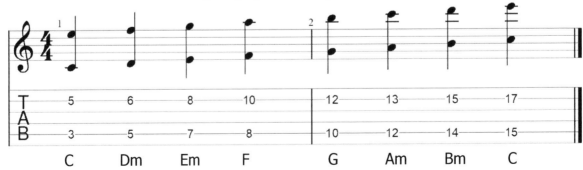

122

...and C Major on the 6th string:

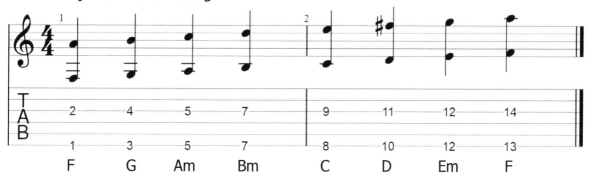

G Major in 10ths:

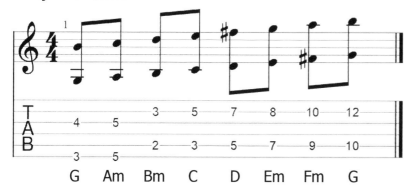

The other cool thing about using the keys of G Major and C Major (keys with none or few ♯'s or ♭'s) is that all open strings become valid notes. Try using some open strings to start constructing melody ideas:

PENTATONICS
OVER CHORDS

Recap

Ok, so we've done a bit of playing pentatonics over chords - here's the recap:

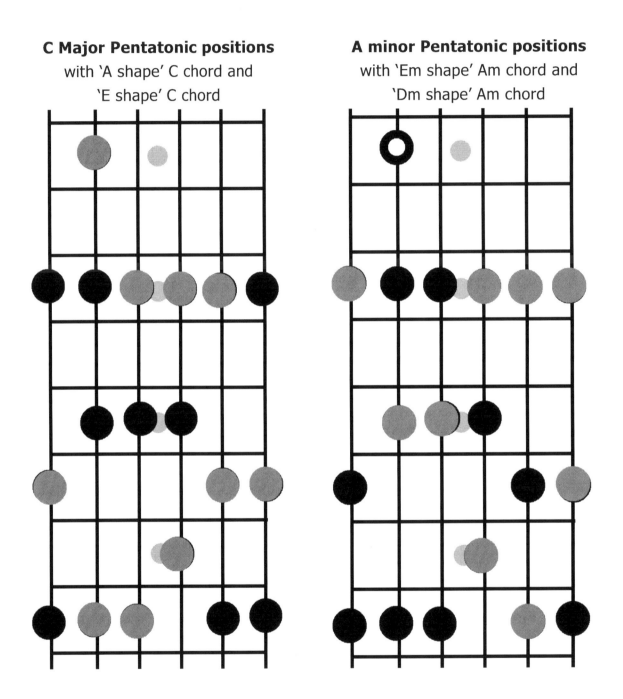

C Major Pentatonic positions
with 'A shape' C chord and
'E shape' C chord

A minor Pentatonic positions
with 'Em shape' Am chord and
'Dm shape' Am chord

We've done E minor and E Major 'shapes' on the 6th string, and we've done an A Major 'shape' on the 5th string. So lets do the minor shape on the 5th string...

Minor Position 4

This is minor Position 4, and as we'll see in a bit, Major position 3.

A minor 'barre' chord at 12 fret

A minor pentatonic at 12th fret.

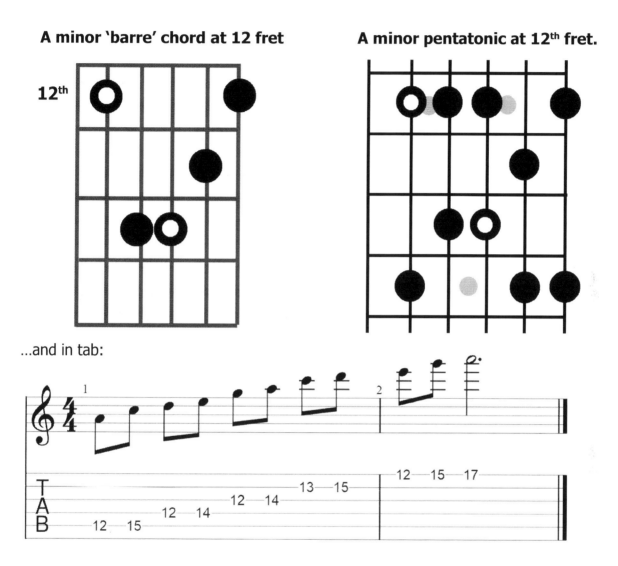

...and in tab:

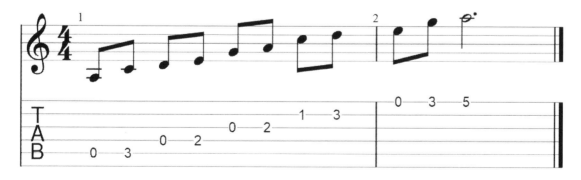

Because we're at our 12th fret we can also look at this in open position:

Major Position 3

So, as we well know by now, every minor hides a Major and every Major conceals a minor, so here's the same shape from the Major perspective. As you'll see this is a great one for the Major scale, very useful indeed.

You'll notice, if you follow the two root notes, they outline a C Major chord. Also, the root note on second string is also the root note of a D 'shape' chord. So really this position is a combination of the C 'shape' and D 'shape' chord.

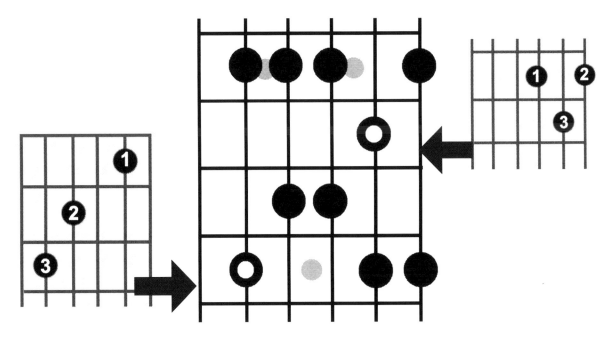

This 'C shape/D shape' chord can be played as one barre chord. Remember they share the root note so they will have the same chord name, here, at 12th fret, it's a C:

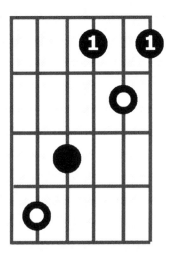

We barre the 1st and 3rd strings with our first finger and fingers 2, 3 and 4 take care of the C shape. Remember this shape is movable. Play this with first finger on the 2nd fret - this gives you a D chord, but a much bigger one than our open position version, or played at 4th fret makes an E chord, and at 5th fret produces an F chord etc. This chord is definitely worth the practice because it fills a hole left by our other chord positions. I often think of it as a 'Goldilocks' chord...

THE GOLDILOCKS CHORD

Sometimes in our barre chord progressions we have a choice between an 'A shape' chords and an 'E shape' chords. For example, if we want to play an E chord we can play an open E, or we have the 7th fret E using an 'A shape' chord. From this opening statement you may already be able to guess the problem. These two chords take up two quite different sonic spaces. The 7th fret position can sound a bit high and the open position can sound too low. This is where our Goldilocks chord can give us some compromise and therefore sound 'just right'.

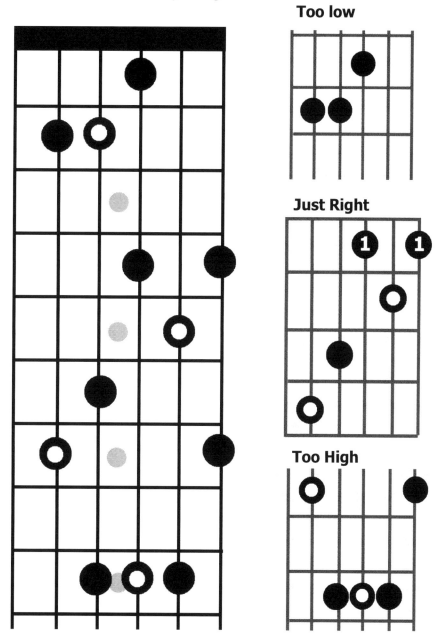

Too low

Just Right

Too High

Minor Blues

Time for a new chord progression to improvise over. We're sticking with the blues theme although this one is a bit more versatile.

We're playing Am Dm F and E

'E?! But E's not in our A minor chord scale!' I hear you point out given that you studied so well in the chord harmony sections. And true you would be. Except minor keys can work a little differently.

Lets get side-tracked

Try this chord progression: |Am |Dm |Em |Am :||

Sounds fine, right?

Yeah, it is. But now try this: |Am |Dm |E |Am :||

See how much more assertive that E Major chord is. That's because it's our V chord, the Dominant chord, when viewed with A minor as our I chord.

Am	Bdim	C	Dm	**Em**	F	G
I	ii	III	iv	**v**	VI	VII

So when in the key of A minor our V chord is also minor so lacks the pull that we like with Dominant chords. It is somewhat a matter of taste, if you want the progression to pull you back to Am you need the E Major chord, if you prefer the more non committed resolution to Am then keep E minor.

The problem with using the E Major chord is that it doesn't fit perfectly with our A minor Pentatonic scale, you can make it work though or you can play an E Major arpeggio over that E chord instead. The 'proper' scale is the **Harmonic minor scale** but that's a subject for another book! For now we'll use what we've got!

The E Major arpeggio will go like this:

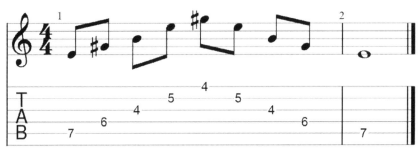

Minor Blues

Ok, so our chord progression was |Am |Dm |F |E |

Play the chords in these positions:

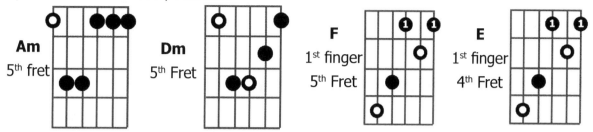

As discussed, we can happily play the minor pentatonic scale over this, mostly, if you're careful, but if you want to consider some 'better' note choices here's some tips:

We can start with the A minor pentatonic 5th fret position, obviously.

The D minor chord change is interesting, you can, and should for the purposes of what we've just done, think about our new position 4 Pentatonic. Because played at 5th fret 5th string it's going to outline our D minor barre chord. Now most of the notes already sit within our A minor pentatonic scale but there is one that doesn't. This is the third of the D minor chord. So playing this note over the D minor chord might sound good, or you may prefer the root, or maybe a small D minor arpeggio.

The F chord, is the relative Major of D minor so we can use the same position again but view it from the Major point of view (position 3, page 128).

We then have that E chord which we will pick some choice arpeggio notes out for.

So we might phrase something like this:

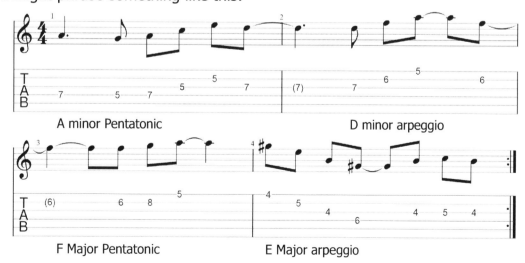

131

WHAT YOU KNOW

The two diagrams below should map out what you now know your fretboard to look like from a minor and Major perspective.

A minor Pentatonic Fretboard

Position 4

Position 1

Position 2

Position 4

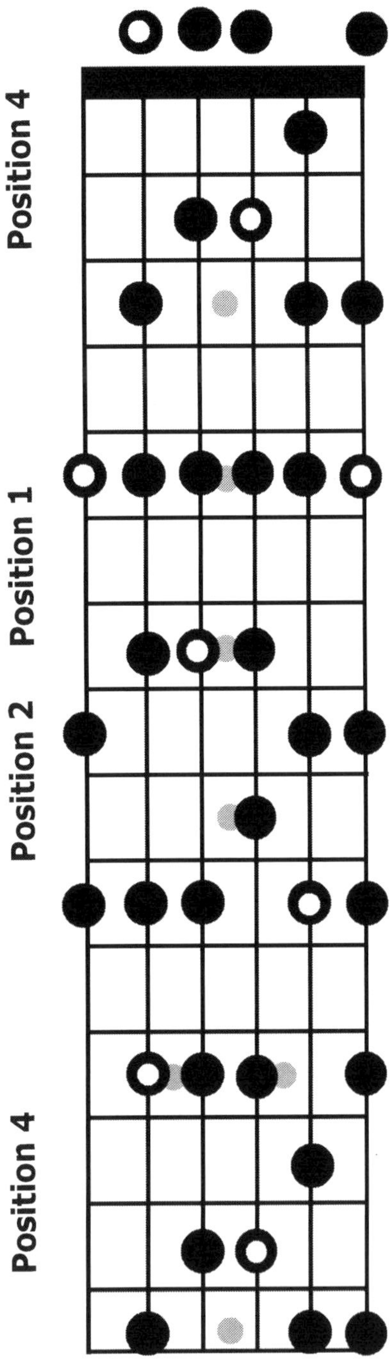

C Major Pentatonic Fretboard

Position 3

Position 5

Position 1

Position 3

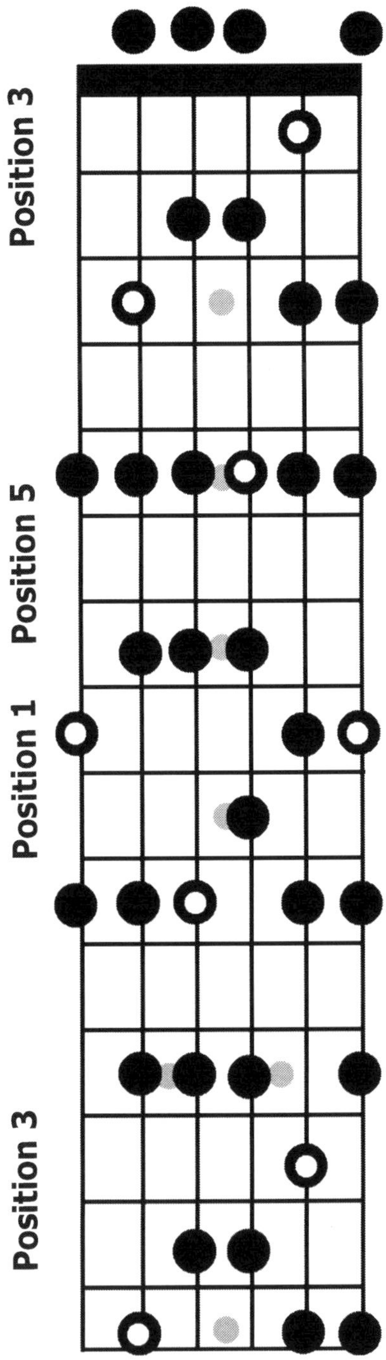

The Invisible Positions

Given the information on the previous fretboard diagrams, you now know all pentatonic positions. However you may notice that from the minor point of view there is a hole between position 2 and position 4 and between position 4 and 1, Or from the Major point of view between positions 1 & 3 and 3 and 5.

This is minor position 5 / Major position 4

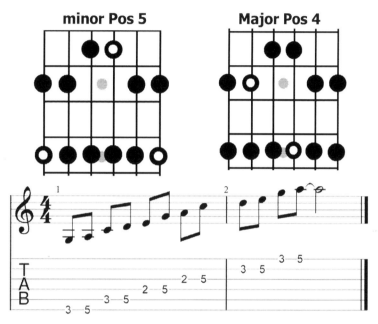

...and this is minor position 3 and Major position 2:

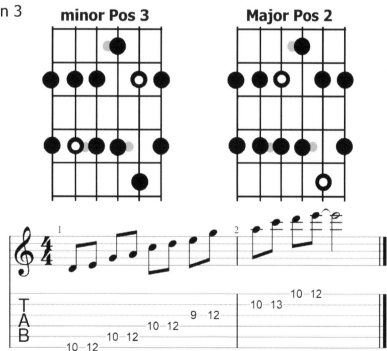

We're going to look at these in more detail shortly, so hold onto your hats!

CAGED
AND THE WHOLE
FRETBOARD

CAGED...

There is a method you may be aware of, or may have heard of, called the **caged system.** If you look at the Major positions on the diagram opposite, you'll see that the order of chords goes 'C shape', 'A shape', G shape, 'E shape' and 'D shape'. What does that spell? CAGED !

Important: Every chord is a C chord.
We're just playing it using different chord shapes.

So hopefully you can see from the diagram we have the pentatonic scale positions and then the CAGED chord that fits into that position. Some chords have a cross-over position, like the A chord fits both into position 5 and position 1, so you can decide to think about this as you like. As long as you can recognise those chords within those scales what we call each position is superfluous to our needs.

Minor Caged

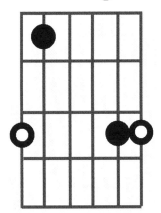

The minor fretboard is a bit different, because we're looking for minor versions of the CAGED chords (p.136)

One that might confuse you is the G minor position because we don't tend to play a G minor in open position and therefore the chord is one that isn't instantly recognisable.

As you can see it's the same as our regular G except the third has been lowered so we have a minor third. This is more helpful as a position guide more-so than a chord, because it's very hard to move and you try barring it!

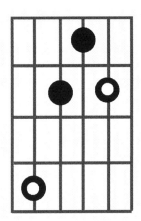

And C minor is just as potentially awkward as a chord. Although definitely more playable than the G minor and it's actually a great arpeggio chord shape. You can see again how the third interval has been flattened to make it a minor chord. I've also added the fifth on the 3rd string in this diagram because these 4 strings can be played together as a movable chord.

CAGED chords on Pentatonic fretboard

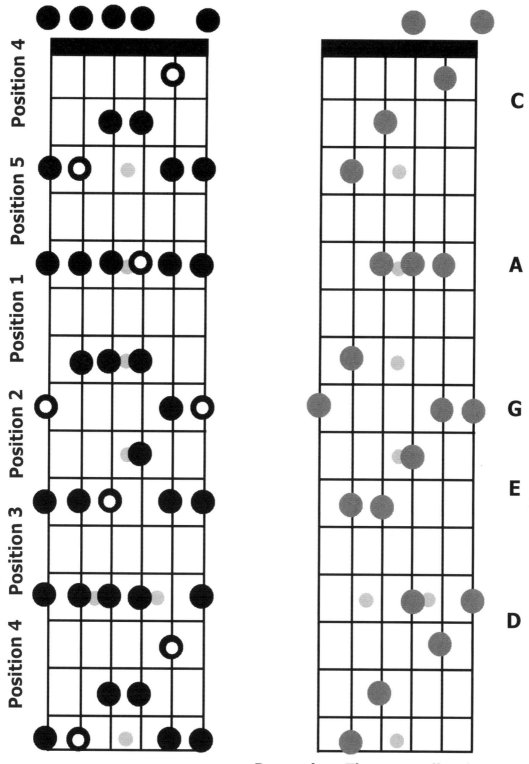

Position 4

Position 5

Position 1

Position 2

Position 3

Position 4

C

A

G

E

D

Remember: These are all C chords.
The names are chord 'shape' references

CAGED minor chords on Pentatonics Fretboard

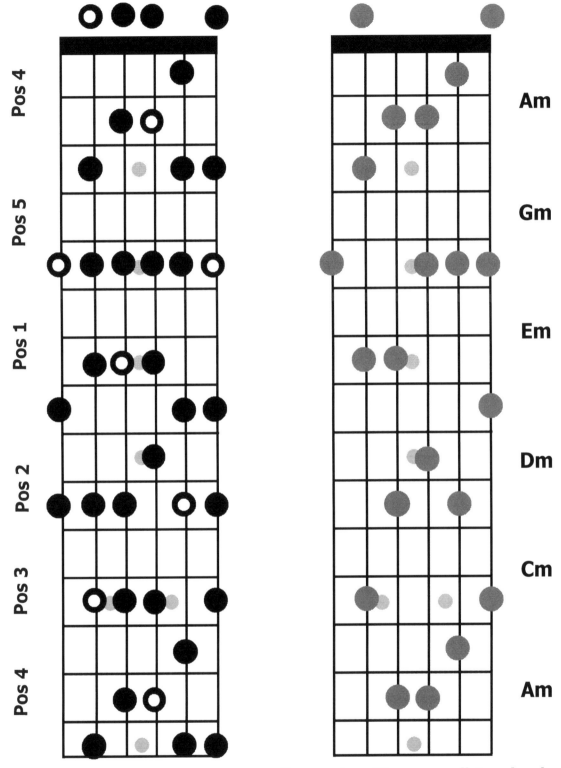

Remember: These are all Am chords.
The names are chord 'shape' references

138

But whether you consider the 'Caged' concept or not you now know your minor and Major pentatonic scales all over the neck! That's actually a big deal, well done!

Remember...

When you are viewing either one of these diagrams you are viewing **one scale.** Just one. We have learned it as many positions because it was easier to digest that way, but when all is said and done how you navigate those notes is up to you.

Also remember, that any time you move a position, for instance you play the D minor chord at 5th fret as we did in the last chapter, the whole fretboard position moves with that chord, these positions are always linked together, always! Whatever the root note is, it all moves according to that root note.

Just for further clarification look at the E minor pentatonic scale over the page.

Hopefully you can see that the left hand side dot patterns are identical whichever scale we're dealing with. It's then just about where you place the root notes and moving the shape accordingly. The chords shapes will reinforce the positions for you and outline your melodic options in your phrasing - this is why chords are so important as lead guitar players - because **chord tones are cool tones**!

CAGED positions in E minor

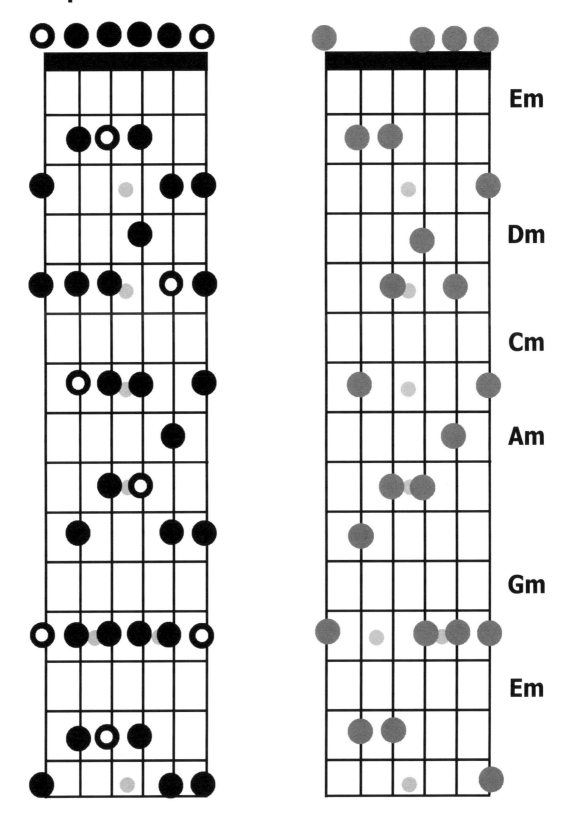

Em

Dm

Cm

Am

Gm

Em

WRONGS NOTES AS RIGHT NOTES

The Blues Scale

So to finish up our work on the pentatonic scales I want to include a few 'outside' notes to spice things up a bit and the first one we're going to look at is the ♭5 note.

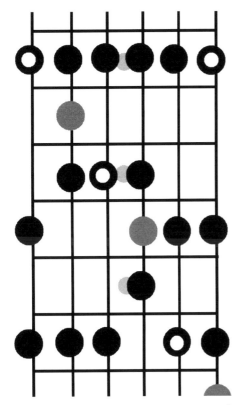

If we label our minor pentatonic in intervals we have R, 3rd, 4th, 5th, 7th. The one we're going to add to create our 'blues' scale is a ♭5 so our scale now has 6 notes R, 3rd, 4th, ♭5th, 5th, and 7th.

It's the chromatic passage between 4, ♭5 and 5 that really give this scale it's sound. The 4 is safe, the ♭5 is really unstable and then we resolve that note to the 5 which is super stable.

You can throw the ♭5 in wherever you fancy it, but more often than not it always wants to resolve to the 5th or the 4th. But it doesn't have to! The only no-no with this is you probably don't want to land on it as a phrase finisher. It's very much a passing through note.

Don't be put off that we call this the 'blues' scale. It really has applications over and above blues music, you can play this anywhere. That ♭5 note is perfect to fit in wherever you feel you want a little bit of chromatic-ism.

Aaaand, while we're here, I thought I'd point out something else that you might like to think about whilst creating your licks, and that's movable shapes.

Movable shapes

We've already seen how we can see our octaves on the neck, but did it occur to you that if the octave has moved then all the notes around the octave are also right there with it?!

Remember that when you reach your 2nd string you need to adjust the shape or octave position by one fret.

Pretty interesting once you see it!

In the diagram I've neglected the 7th just to make the positions a bit easier to visualise but obviously do include it if you want it, like this:

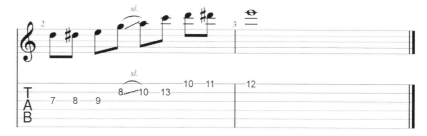

It's a very useful mechanism for creating runs and 'shreddy' lines, perhaps less functional when thinking melodically. But definitely a great visualisation tool.

Licks

Here are some licks to practice the sound of the ♭5 with.

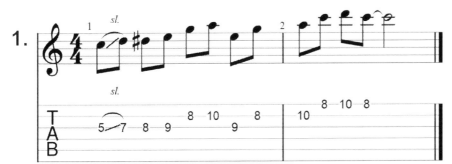

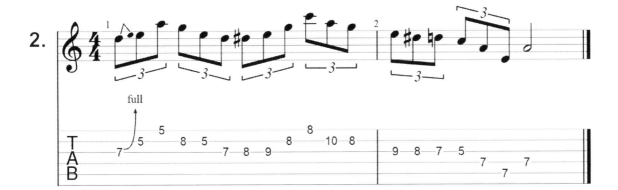

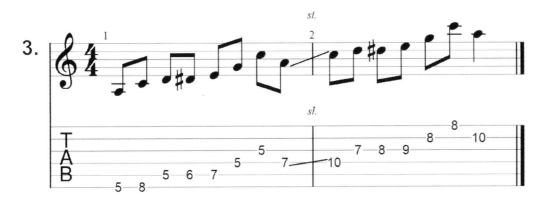

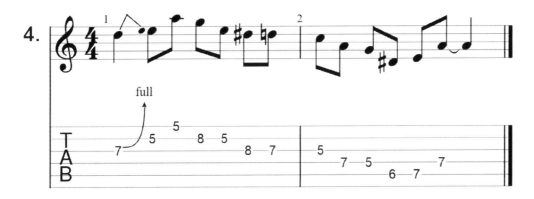

3rd and Flat 3rd

Here's another idea that we can utilise in our pentatonic improvising. Going from the ♭3 to the Major 3. We've sort of already looked at this when combining Major and minor pentatonics over the blues progression. This is a little different though because we're combining them into one scale this time instead of thinking specifically of a Major scale or a minor scale. Our home base will be the minor scale for these examples because as we saw before it's more musically malleable than the Major scale.

We'll start with our A minor pentatonic position and add the Major 3rd to it:

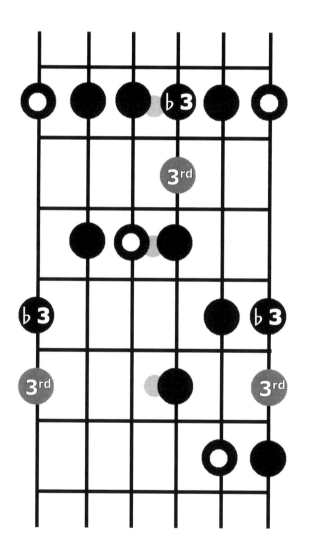

Once again the best way to visualise this is to see the chord. You should be able to now see that we have a minor 'E shape' barre and a Major 'E shape' barre stacked in the same diagram, right? The Major 3rd being the 3rd of the E shape. Or, if you look at the 'D minor shape' position, the 3rd creates a D Major shape chord.

Just like the ♭5, this works best when used as a either a chromatic flourish or over the **Root Major** chord to accentuate the Major even though we're primarily thinking minor.

Also please remember this is only showing one position. Be aware of where your 3rds around your neck and it'll open up other lick possibilities - always be thinking chords shapes.

♭ 3 to 3 Licks

1.
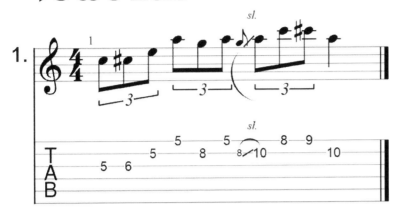

2.
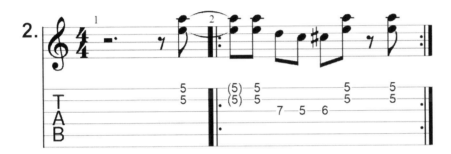

3.

Use in in your rhythm riffs too:

4.
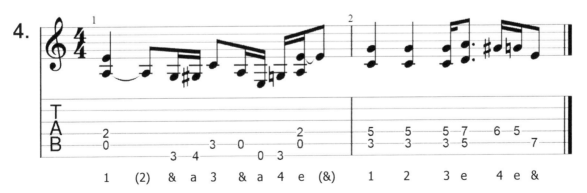

146

Combine them

I mean, why wouldn't you?!

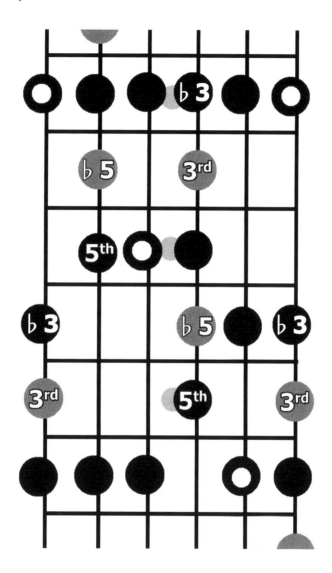

Combined lick example:

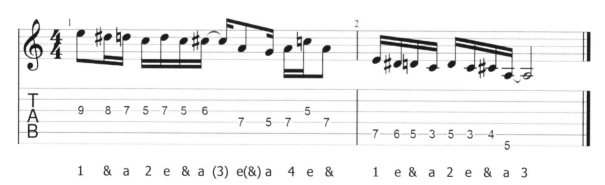

HELP! MY FINGERS DON'T WORK!

FINGER FITNESS

There are lots of finger fitness routines that people have invented. These are some of my favourites.

Playing anything using each finger is always beneficial, this exercise is huge but focuses on each pair of fingers in every combination. **Play each 4 note pattern up and down each string -** I've put in the arrow to remind you to do this. Then move to the next bar and do the same.

First finger start

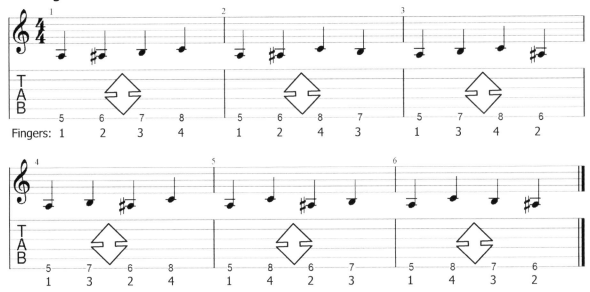

Second finger start

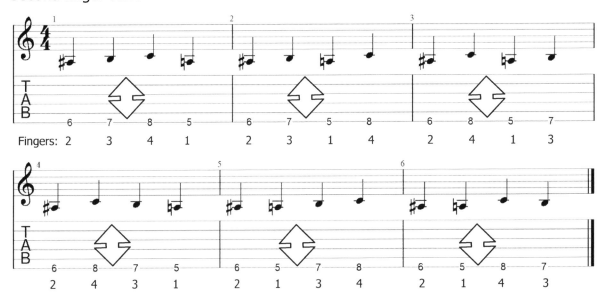

150

Third finger start

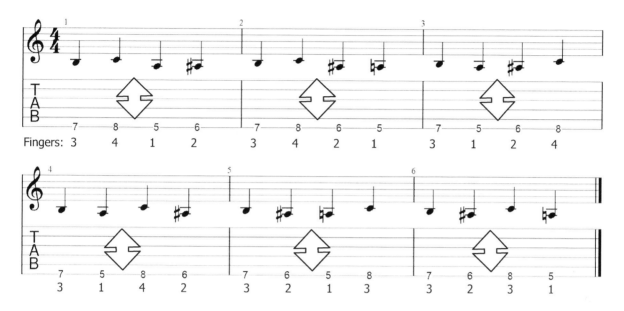

Fourth finger start

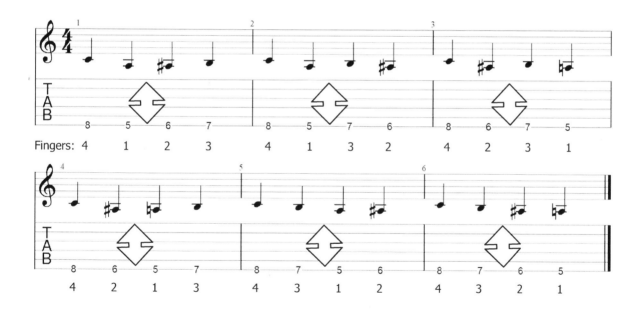

Yeah, it's a big one, but it's very good. When I do finger exercises I tend to try and do them when doing something else - I mean, not like when I'm gardening - but maybe when I'm watching a film - that's a great time to practice these kinds of things.

Here is a good chromatic scale exercise that needs good picking skills and finger dexterity to pull of accurately.

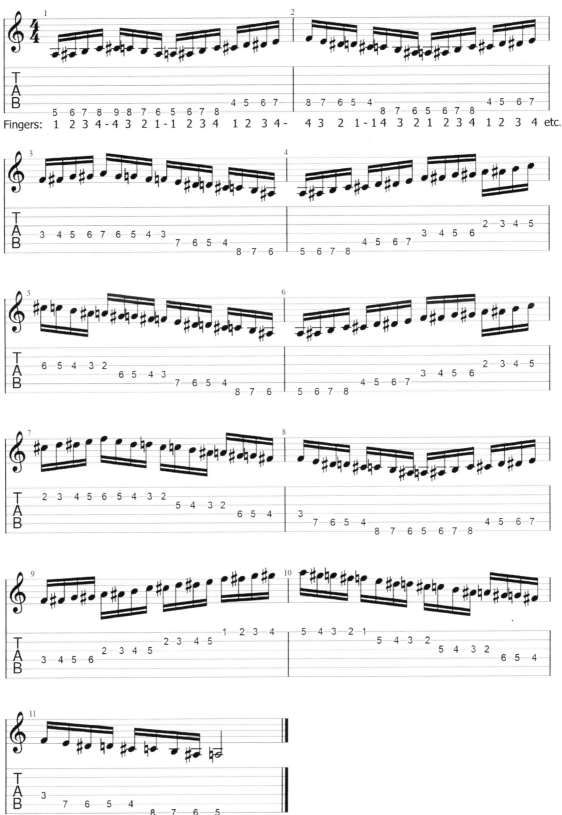

More...

If you want something a little quicker and milder then this is a good option that makes you focus on moving each finger individually.

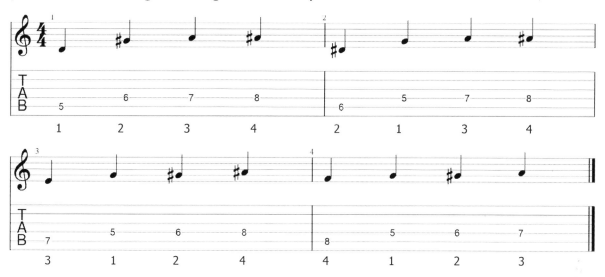

This next one is good for finger placement and also a good picking exercise:

And this one:

And now, the most hideous sounding practice routine known to man…

….It's good though. See how hard it is to accurately land on all those adjacent strings. Just practice it quietly so people don't think you've gone deranged!

Hopefully these will liven up those sloppy fingers for you. Remember to play everything slowly at first, your fingers won't learn good motion and placement if you don't practice good motion and placement, so keep them slow and absolutely nail them!

SEVENTH HEAVEN

SEVENTH CHORDS

Before we look at some shapes let's figure out what a 7th chord is and why we use them.

As we know, our 'regular' chords have 3 notes. We call these three notes a **triad**. Those notes are the Root, third and fifth. When we make 7th chords we add the 7th to that sequence. Easy right?! There is one small thing we have to be aware of though, and that's that we have two types of 7th's . Let me explain...

Let's take our C Major scale and start constructing some chords.

C	D	E	F	G	A	B
1	2	3	4	5	6	7

For our C (7th) chord we take the R, 3, 5, and 7th that gives us the notes **C E G B** When we put these notes together we get a C **Major 7th** chord. Now, this next bit is important. We call it a **Major 7th**, not because it's a Major chord, but because the 7th is derived from the Major scale and therefore it's a **Major 7th**. This is because the 7th note - the B - is only 1 fret away from the C root. Keep that in mind as we do the rest.

We know the next two chords are minor chords, but lets look at the 7th note. Our D chord is made up of D F A and C, 1 3 5 and 7. But this time the 7th is a whole step - two frets - away from the D Root. We call this a **7th** - unlike with the C chord which we called a **Major 7th**.

When naming 7th chords we always assume a non minor chord to be a Major, so we will call a C Major a C. We will call a D minor a D minor still because we need to distinguish the 3rd of the chord to be minor. We then add the **type of 7th** to the name. So with the C chord we have a **Major 7th** i.e. the **Major 7th** is next to the root. C **Major 7**. With D minor we have a **7th** - the **7th** is two frets from the root. Dm**7**. See the difference? Lets continue.

Our E minor chord is also an E minor **7th** just like the Dm7. Our IV chord is an F **Major 7th** just like our I chord, the C **Major 7th**. Now the reason we need to distinguish these 7th's is because our V chord is different. Our V chord is a G7 chord. This is a Major chord. But the 7th - the F - is two frets away from the G so it's not a **Major 7th** its just a

7th. So we call it G**7**. Also, because it's our V chord and these are our **Dominant** chords we can call it a **Dominant 7th.** Lets look at some shapes...

A Shapes

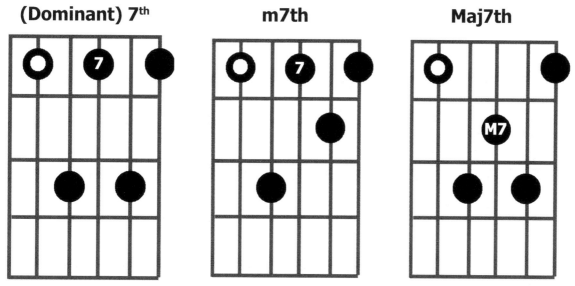

Here you can see exactly how the 7th's sit in the chord. With the 7th and minor 7th its a whole step from where the root note would be and in the Maj 7th its right next to where the root note would be. Remember with Major chords the 7th only occurs on our V chord - our Dominant. Our I and IV chords are Maj7ths.

E Shapes

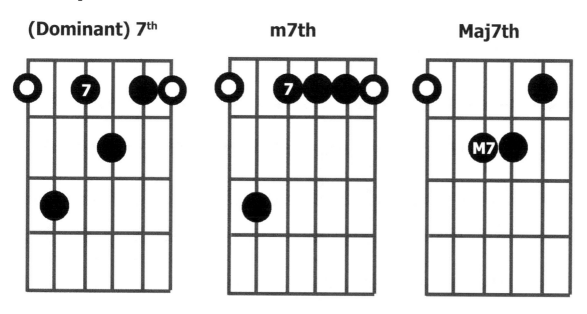

7th Chord scale

Just before we get to the chord scale we need to address the seventh 7th chord in our chord scale - the **half-diminished*** chord.

This used to be called our diminished chord but once we add a 7th to it it becomes a, wait for it, **minor** (♭3) **7** (two frets from the root) ♭**5** (flat 5). So in the C Major chord scale its a **Bm7** ♭**5** and we play it like this:

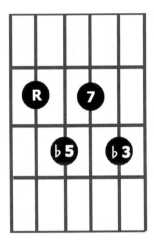

This is our 'A shape' position. Imagine if you un-flatted the 5th you'd have a m7 chord shape, and if you un-flatted the 3rd too you'd have a regular A shape 7 barre chord.

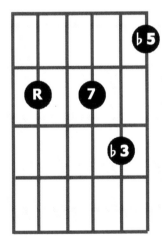

We can also play it with the ♭5th on the 1st string like this. You need to mute the D string on this one with your middle (Root note) finger.

Just to make everything make musical sense, lets do one of our chord scales again so you can hear how these 7th notes move and add to our overall harmony.

So our new C Major chord sequence is

CM7   Dm7   Em7   FM7   G7   Am7   Bm7 ♭**5   (CM7)**

*In a true 4 note diminished chord the intervals are all m3rd's apart so we'd have R ♭3 ♭5 6 - because this one has the 7th is only a half-diminished - in case you wondered!

C Major 4 note chord scale

Here's the C Major scale using 'A shape' 7th chords.

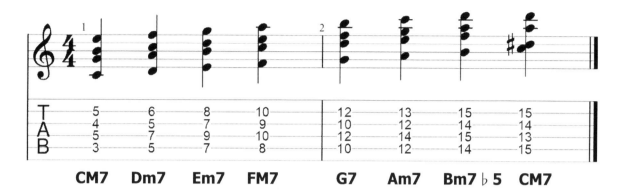

Lets Jazz!

Now lets mix up our A shapes with some E shapes.

A common chord progression in Jazz, but not strictly Jazz, is the ii V I progression.

In C Major that's **Dm7 G7 CM7** and we'll play it thus:

| Dm7 | G7 | CM7 | CM7   :||

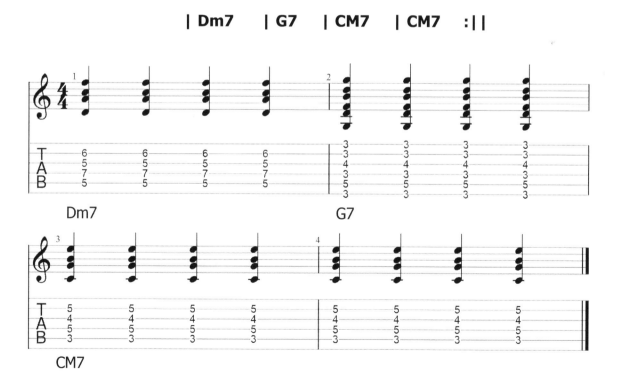

Not all M7 are M7's

Once more when dealing with blues inspired music we hit a conundrum when dealing with 7th chords. We've just seen that if we played a I7 IV7 V7 progression in C Major our chords would be CM7, FM7 and G7 - That's literally what I've just told you. However, take a I IV V in A like we did in the improvisation section and play each chord as the correct 7th chord. So the A will be AM7 the D is DM7 and the E is E7:

Hmmm.... Sounds sort of funny right? It's fine, everything is good, you could write a song that does that... but the vibe just doesn't vibe 'blues'.

So what a traditional Blues does differently is use **Dominant 7's** on **every** chord.

Therefore our A blues progression is A7 D7 and E7. Sounds much better, at least it sounds more 'blues' right?!

Remember how we said that the minor scale works just fine over these Major chords. This is partly because whilst these chords have a Major 3rd, they also have a ♭7, relatively speaking, rather than the Major 7th, therefore the same 7th that's in our minor pentatonic scale.

Before moving on I would highly encourage you to record some backing tracks for dominant I IV V's and also for the ii V I and improvise over them using your pentatonic shapes.

ARPEGGIOS FOR 7ᵀᴴ CHORDS

These are 'A shape' 7ᵗʰ arpeggios written with C Roots.

Up first is the 'Dominant' 7 arpeggio. You can see in the fretboard diagram you have a choice of 3ʳᵈ depending whether you like to stretch your fingers or not.

or

This is a C Major 7ᵗʰ arpeggio. We have the same 3ʳᵈ note choice as above.

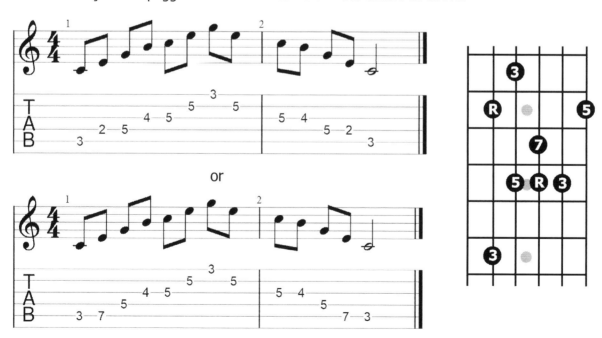

or

161

And here is the 'A shape' minor 7th arpeggio.

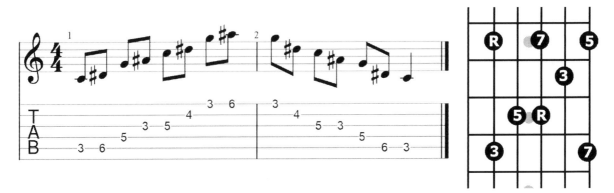

'E shape' 7th arpeggios

For the 'E shape' arpeggios we've put the root on the A note so this first one is the A Dominant 7 arpeggio. Just like with the 'A shape' you can choose your 3rd.

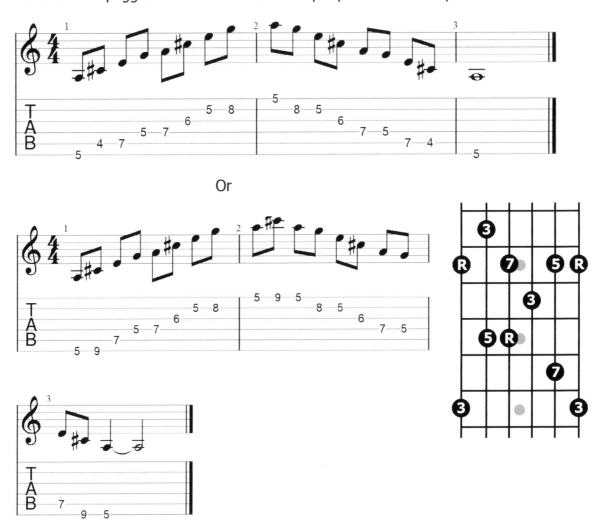

Or

Next up, the 'E shape' Major 7th and as usual you can choose your 3rd depending on if you like to stretch your fingers or not… but also we can choose a stretchy 7th to go with the 3rd, or feel free to mix them up.

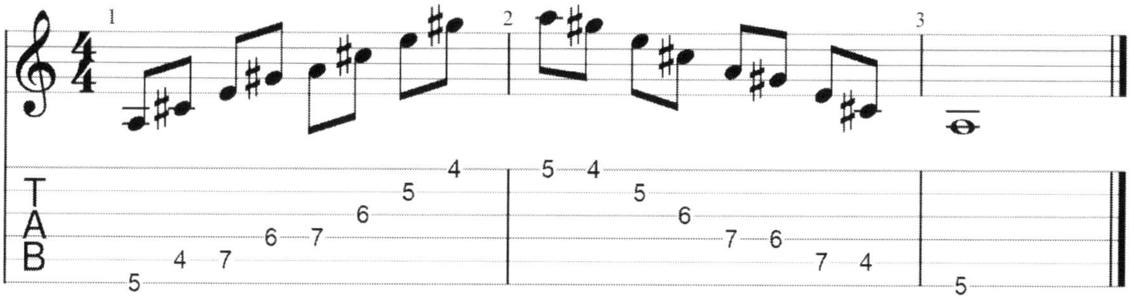
TAB

Or

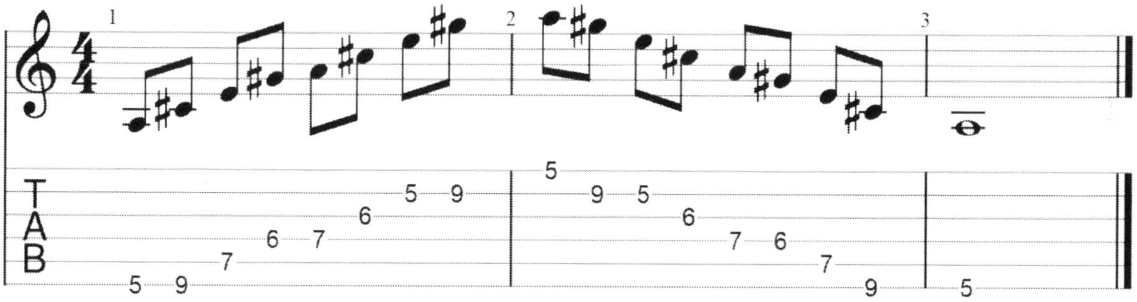
TAB

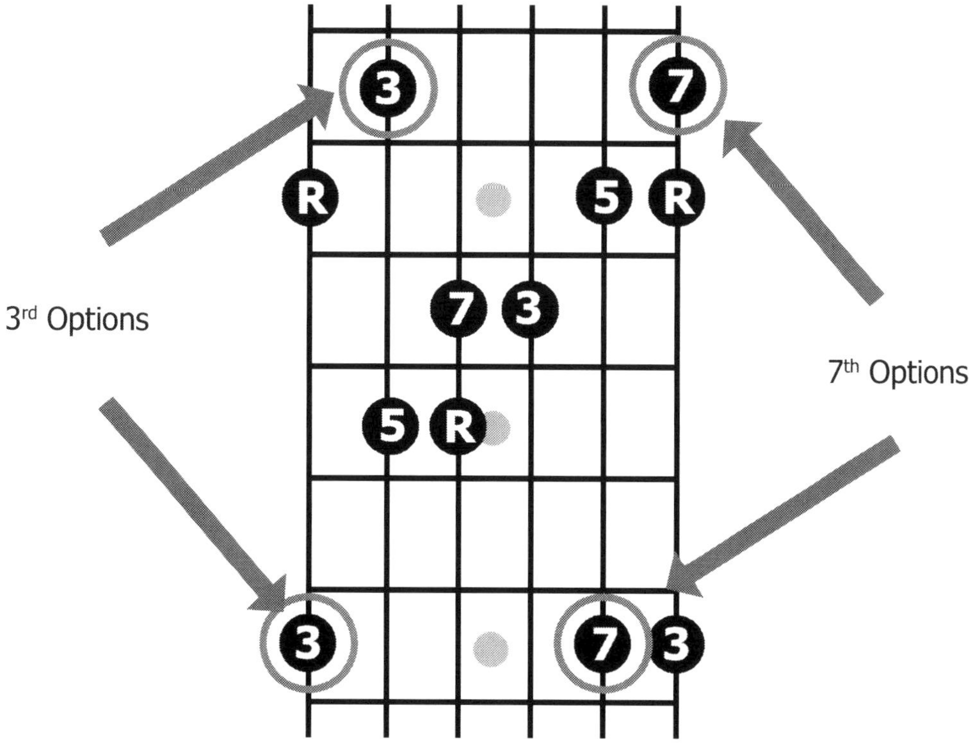
3rd Options
7th Options

....And the minor 7th 'E shape'

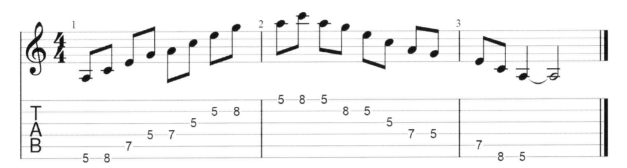

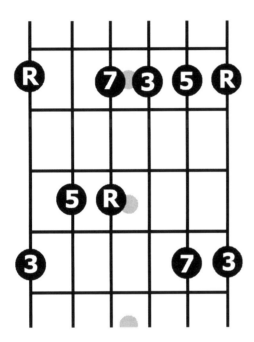

Remember the point!

Just like with any arpeggio, the point is not necessarily to play them up and down as fast as possible (although that can be cool!) We use them as visual guides and melodic patterns that allow us to play the 'good notes' over chords. You don't always have to play the same arpeggio as the chord. Try playing a C Major arpeggio over an A minor chord or an F Major arpeggio over a C chord, there are lots of great arpeggio over chord ideas that sound cool, but more of this a bit later.

The Goldilocks 7th Chord

Remember we looked at the C shape 'Goldilocks' chord? Here's the same idea but with the added 7th. This is a Dominant chord because the 7th is a ♭7 compared to the Major scale. You may also notice there is no 5th interval. The 5th would be the open string on a open C chord where we now have the 7th note. As we've seen previously, the 5th in no way defines a chord, so we're quite happy to go without it on this occasion.

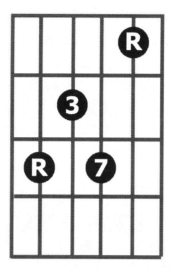

This is a good chord to keep our 7th I IV V progressions in one place because it allows you to play all three chord at your 5th fret.

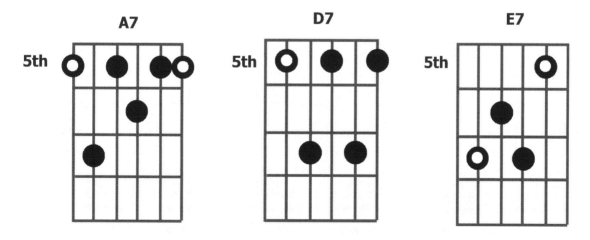

Not that you have to play them all at your 5th fret! You could use the C7 shape at 3rd fret for the D and then move the shape up to the 5th fret for the E7.

New Blues

Here's a new 12 bar Blues progression to try incorporating the C7 shape. Try this one really slow, around 60bpm, for that authentic slow blues feel.

|Am7 |Am7 |Am7 |Am7 |Dm7 |Dm7 |
|Am7 |Am7 |F7 |E7 |Am7 Dm7|Am7 E7 :||

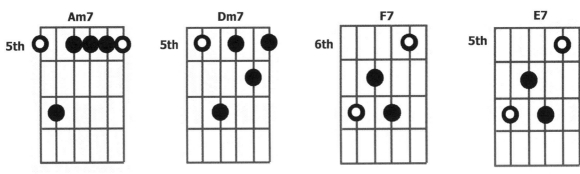

C7 Arpeggio

With new chords come new arpeggios, so here is a position that you could use to cover the 'C7 Goldilocks' position.

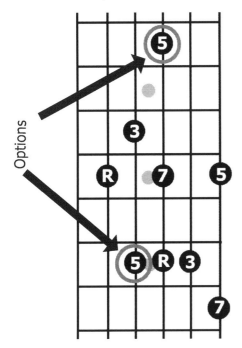

Being a Dominant 7th chord you can play any dominant 7 arpeggio over each chord as described on the previous pages. I particularly like this position (actually 2 positions) though:

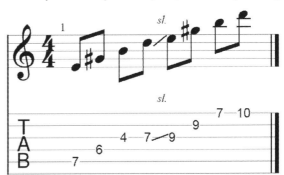

It's follows the chord well and it flirts nicely with the minor pentatonic 1st position.

Obviously over the F7 chord everything moves up one note, so the root is an F, right! The cool thing about the F7 arpeggio is that you naturally get to use the b5 in the arpeggio. Nice!

Improvisation Guidelines

Ok, this one is a bit trickier. There are a few more traps that can befall you and concepts that can be taken too far. So far we know is pretty safe to play a minor pentatonic over a blues, but there can be a couple of 'not the best' note choices on the chord changes. We can correct this by thinking of the chord change and either playing the new chord as a pentatonic or arpeggio to solves this crisis... to a degree. Now with these two new 'out of key' changes - the E7 and F7 - we have to be even more careful, and yet sometimes just playing the arpeggio over them, which should work fine because it's just the notes of the chord, can just sound... well... Meh!

So why is that? There is a thing called musical memory. At least that's what I call it. It's the concept of how a blues needs to sound like the blues. If there are too many odd notes or changes, whilst you could argue that they are good notes, they don't fulfil the mood of the piece and can in fact detract from the feel and sound a little odd in the context.

Keep in mind that when you play a blues in A minor pentatonic for instance, that the minor pentatonic sound is 'the sound' of the song. The other notes that we might use that fall outside of this - like the minor 3rd of the D minor chord, the R and 7 of the F7 chord and 3rd of the E7 chord - we have to use these notes to good effect to highlight the changes but not to detract from the overall A minor pentatonic sound. Think of these as contrast notes - highlight the chord and get out of there, or use them as alternative landing notes whilst maintaining focus on the A minor pentatonic.

For inspiration for this type of progression it'll be worth listening to 'The Thrill has gone' by BB King and 'Story of the Blues' by Gary Moore.

Bring on the Big Boys!

THE MAJOR SCALE

We've played it in open position, we've used it to figure out chords, and we've used it to create chord progressions... It's time we delved a little deeper to figure out exactly how useful this thing is...

Lets start by Placing your chord scale on the neck. But instead of doing it horizontally across the neck lets stack the chords in one position.

As usual lets approach this in C Major. For instance, as if you needed reminding by now, we take our C, Dm, Em, F, G , Am, Bdim chords in one position. Lets do them around 5th-8th fret position. So Major position 5.

Be aware that these are not necessarily the best options for playing these chords, we're just using them as visual aids for what comes next.

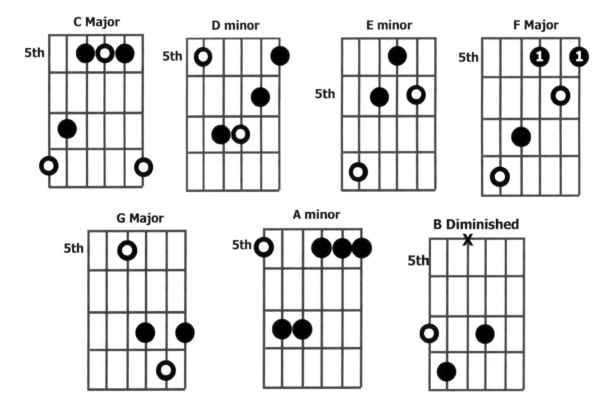

On the next page we're going to stack these chords on top of each other, one at a time, to form a composite scale - the Major scale. Logic would suggest that as each chord is made up from 1, 3, 5 intervals of the Major scale once stacked they will give us the full Major scale position.

170

Chord

Composite Scale

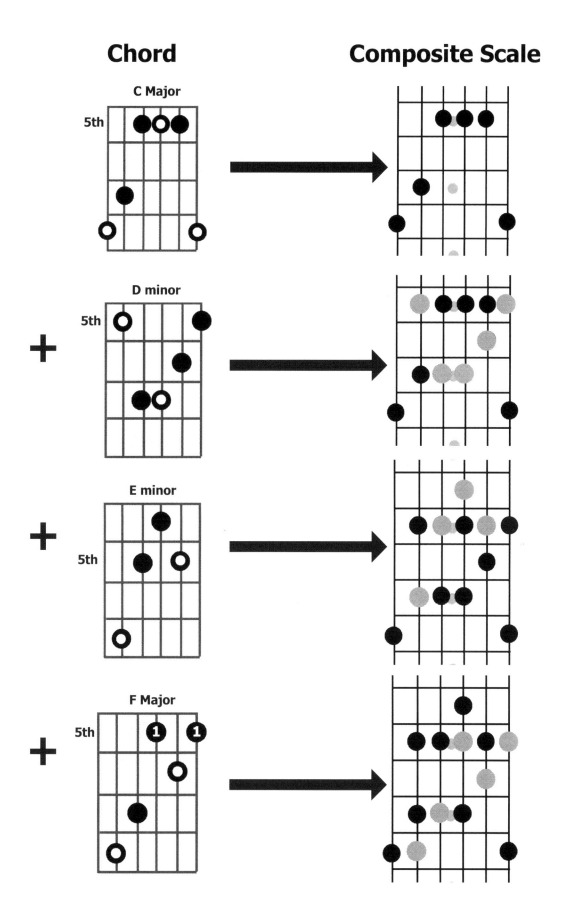

Chord

Composite Scale

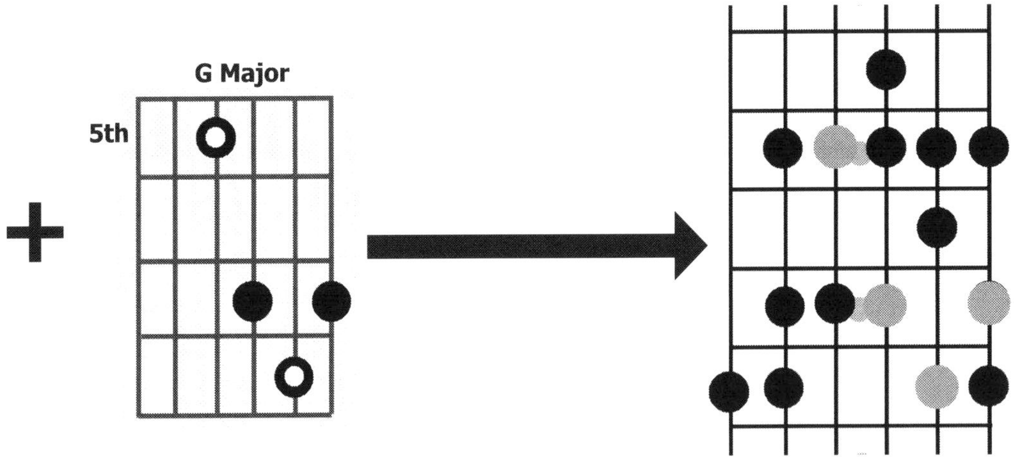

G Major

5th

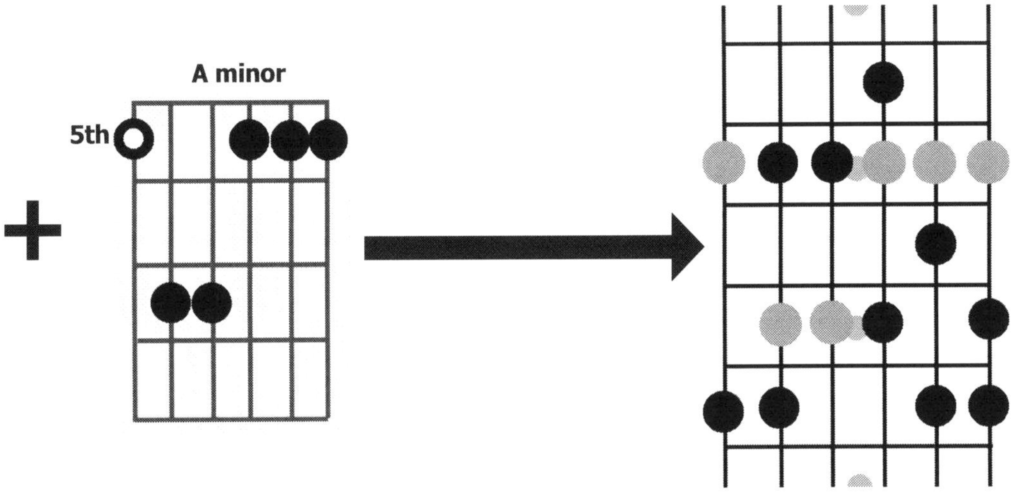

+

A minor

5th

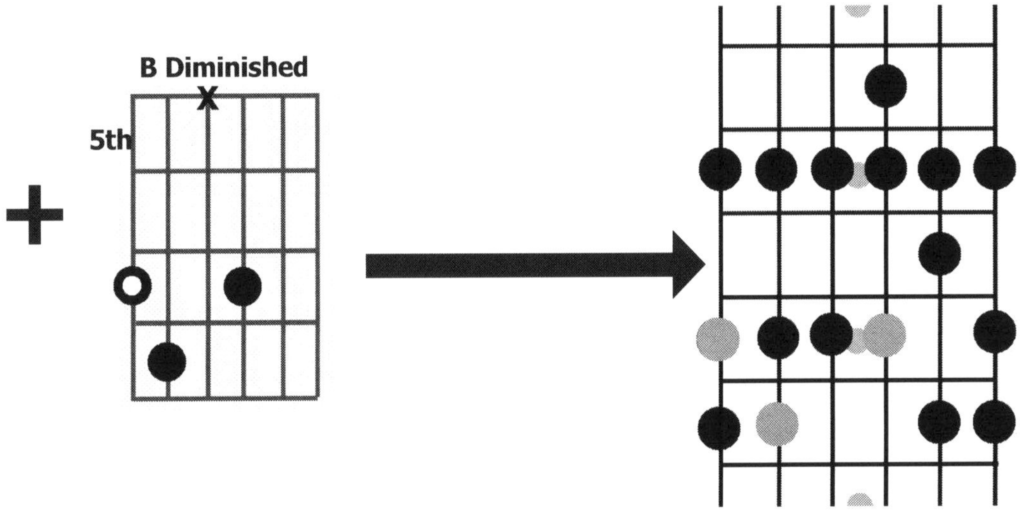

+

B Diminished

5th

+

The Major Scale

So here it is, position 5 of the Major scale.

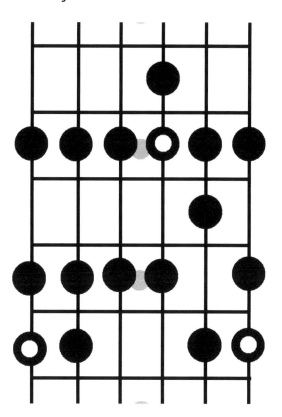

It shouldn't look too unfamiliar to you as it's basically the same as the pentatonic scale but with two extra notes, an F note and a B note. Although because the scale covers just over two octaves it looks like 5 extra notes.

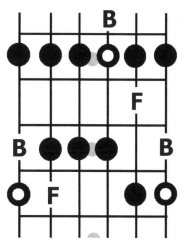

When played from Root to Root you will hear that all too familiar Major scale which brings us right back to where we actually started this book! That's progress for you!

And remember that for each Major scale there is the minor relative...

173

Natural Minor Scale

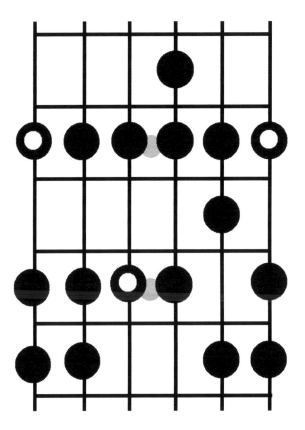

We call this scale the **Natural minor scale**. There are other minor scales, but that's a subject for another time.

As with the Major point of view this should look very familiar to you as, once again, it's basically the same as the pentatonic scale but with the F and a B notes.

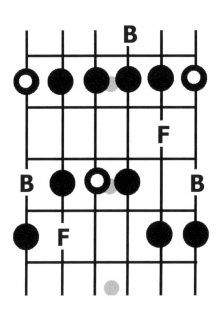

Stairway to Heaven(ly Notes)

So why do we need this scale? Good question. Apart from everything we've already covered about understanding the chords and notes that make keys with which we write songs, when improvising people enjoy thinking with just one scale. Rather than thinking about what chord we are playing over, finding a pentatonic scale or chordal arpeggio and then playing that, people enjoy having one shape with all the notes and then 'feeling' their way through the chord progressions.

Now, this 'feeling' your way through a progression is valid. But unfortunately is also the reason people get stuck in a rut and don't learn to follow chord patterns. This is why we've left it until this late in the book to cover it! But now you know how to hear and follow chords and progressions we can now condense that information into this one position. Just to demonstrate why this can be more beneficial to using our pentatonics, take the solo from Stairway to Heaven. The chord progression is Am G and F.

Using the A Natural minor scale you could play this:

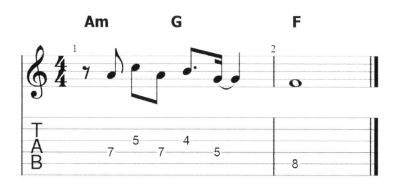

In this example we've played the A root and the minor third over the Am. Over the G we played the B note, which doesn't exist in our pentatonic but is in the G chord, and we also get to land on an F note over the F chord which also doesn't appear in our pentatonic. But rather than consider it as a sequence of chord tones or separate pentatonic scales we just played one scale and let our ears decide the best notes for the chord changes.

Stairway To Heaven uses the same chord progression but plays a pentatonic phrase over the Am and G chords descending to the F note over the F chord.

To do this effectively you do need to be very aware of your chord changes, but using the one position can be useful in giving you all the good notes literally at your fingertips!

Comfortably Done

For the next improvised example lets take a chord progression similar to the Pink Floyd classic Comfortably Numb. We call this a **descending chord cliché** and it can be heard in lots of other songs. From the Major point of view, we are descening the chords in order: vi V IV (iii) ii back to vi (if you can think of this vi as minor Root I it makes even more logical sense!) We're using the chords Bm A G (F♯/D) Em Bm. The F♯ (3rd of D) behaves more as a passing tone here, but you could play either the F♯ note or if you fancy putting the iii chord in that works too. By contrast the Stairway progression is simpler just using the descending vi V VI chords. This is an even more common chord progression idea particularly when working in minor key.

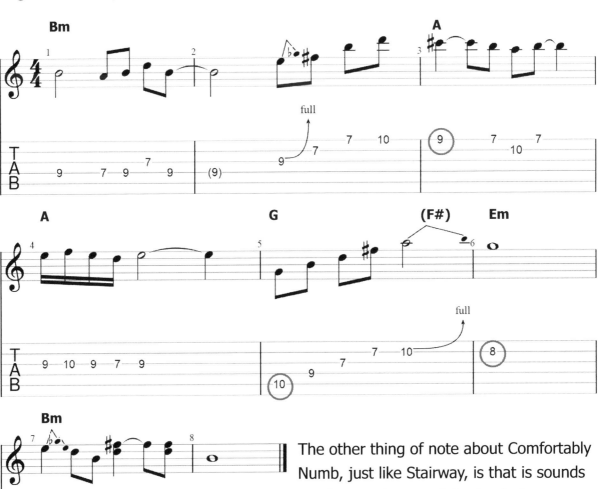

The other thing of note about Comfortably Numb, just like Stairway, is that is sounds good as a minor pentatonic - but sometimes you just want to add those other 'tasty notes', which is where our natural minor comes in.

In this improvised example you'll see this is mostly B minor pentatonic with a few exceptions that coincide with the chord changes - or the 'tasty notes' as I call them. I've circled these notes for your convenience and you will notice that they all fall outside of the pentatonic scale but they are all included in the Natural minor scale because they are all chord tones. It is important with this kind of song that we keep the minor pentatonic tonality and just sprinkle the 'tasty notes' around sparingly. If you strictly followed each chord with a pentatonic shape or arpeggio you could easily lose the feel of the piece.

Iron Maiden

For our last example of the Natural minor scale lets look at another very common use of this chord sequence.

This time we start on the vi we're going to go to the IV and then to the V. We're going to do this in G Major / E minor.

|Em | | C | | D | | Em | ||

This is a fairly typical old school Iron Maiden type progression that was very popular in the 80's in this genre.

It helps if you play this one with the Iron Maiden gallop:

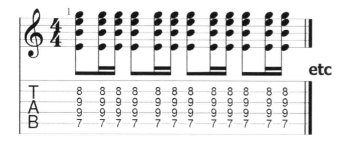

For this I would play all the chords using 5th string Root therefore starting at 7th for the E minor go to 3rd for the C and then 5th fret for the D.

Contrary to this, when we solo we want to stay as close to one position as possible and milk our scale possibilities.

On the next page you will see our E Natural minor scale with the C chord 'Tasty notes' mapped out. Remember we're still playing the E minor scale. These note will flavour

**E Natural minor
with C chord**

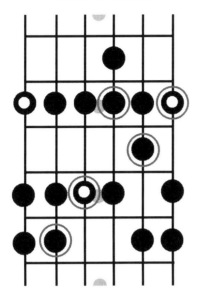

the chord change to pull the listeners ear into the chord. You will continue to think E minor over the C chord, just use the notes to add definition to the chord if you feel its required.

You will also use the same idea over the D chord...

**E Natural minor
with D chord**

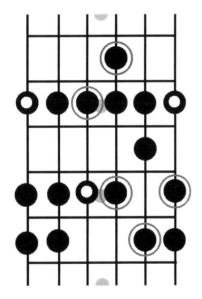

Here's the D chord outlined in the E Natural minor scale. Remember we're still thinking E minor pentatonic / natural minor but these notes will bring the D chord to life if used wisely.

Of course with this chord progression you could actually just play chord arpeggios over each chord, which is quite stylistically acceptable with this genre of music and can also sounds killer. Remember all your tools that you've learned up to this point are still valid and it's a great chord progression for trying out everything with.

Check out the example on the next page for a musical example of this style.

Note this time I've included the rhythm guitar line on top too:

|Em | | C | | D | | Em | ||

Have fun!

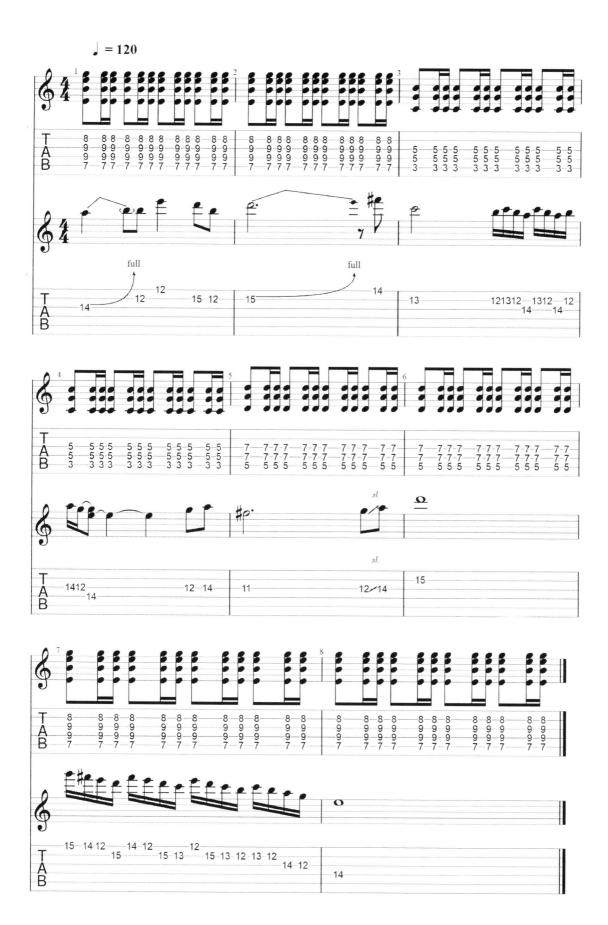

179

THE BIGGEST FRETBOARD DIAGRAM IN THE WORLD EVER...

(NOT REALLY)

So many dots!

On the opposite page you've probably noticed the ridiculous array of dots that you now have to learn. It's the Natural Minor scale in A minor and the C Major scale covering your entire neck - at least until until the point where your neck repeats itself.

My approach with learning this diagram would be to first visually compare it to your pentatonic fretboard that we did on page 135, 136 - its exactly the same information we've just added 2 dots to each position. Then whether you prefer the sound of your Major scale or your minor scale start looking to play that scale in each position. I'd go with the Major scale personally, because it's so familiar sounding it's easier for most people to spot mistakes when playing. So for instance you might play this:

This is a great exercise that you really should get to grips with. Playing a Major scale from any note is actually a pretty useful skill to have. Use the diagram to guide you for a bit and then see if you can do it yourself by using your ear alone.

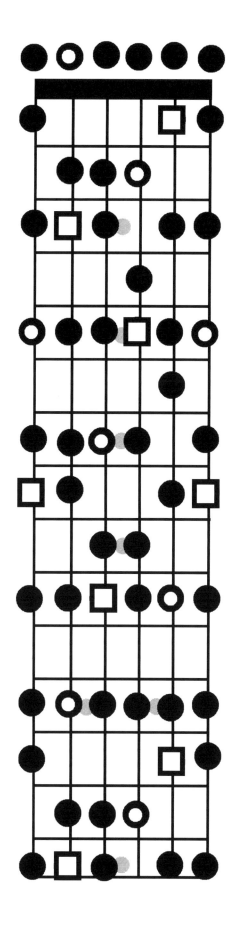

○ **Natural minor Root**

□ **Major scale Root**

A minor, everywhere

Here's the same exercise at the C Major one we just did but with playing the A Natural minor in all positions:

Simplifying

Now there are clearly a lot of ways we can think about navigating all these notes. But I'd like to visually simplify things a bit first.

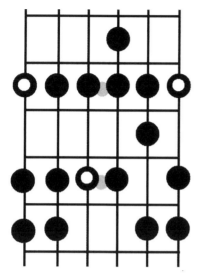

First of all we're going to focus on our 6th string A minor position that we did in the previous chapter:

No problems here.

Always visualise these as the pentatonic skeletons you're used to but with a bit more meat on their bones - the extra two notes.

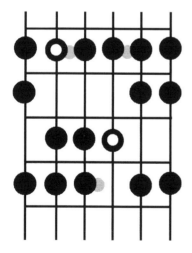

Our 5th string root version is played from our 12th fret, as you know.

As usual visualise its root notes, the pentatonic framework, and see the minor arpeggio / chord shape embedded in there too.

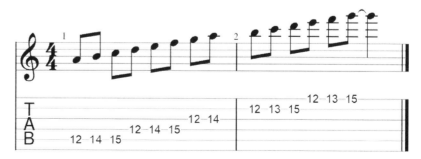

Now comes the sneaky bit. We can play a 3 note per string C Major scale to bridge the gap between these two 'minor' positions to really open up the possibilities.

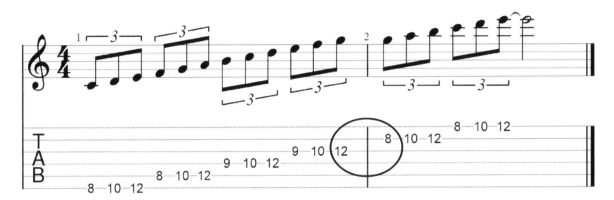

What you may have noticed is that when playing through the position we have two of the same notes together. We're going to ignore this, after all we're looking at it from a 'visualising / shape' point of view more so than trying to get a perfect scale.

However, the double note can actually lead to some pretty cool licks ideas!

Hopefully you can see how symmetrically beautiful this position is:

...and how it perfectly fits between our two minor positions.

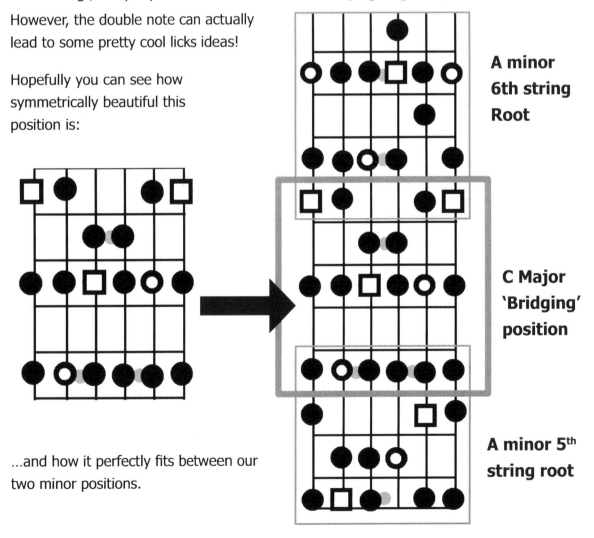

A minor 6th string Root

C Major 'Bridging' position

A minor 5th string root

Add a dash of Major...

Add to this a 2 octave 3rd fret C Major scale:

...and this should help you grasp and recognise A minor and C Major over the vast majority of your neck.

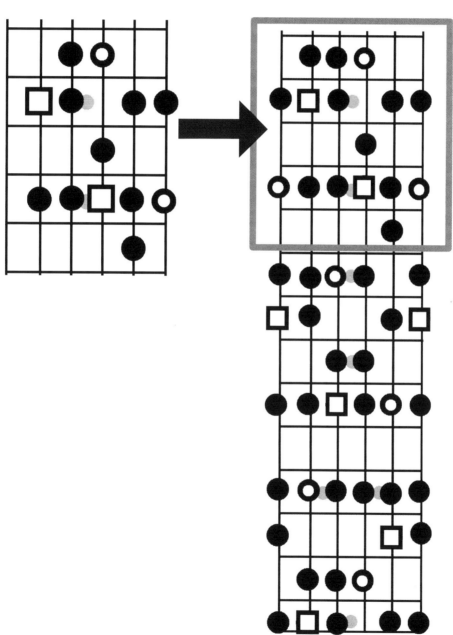

Guitar Tetris

Another way you may like to view these fretboard shapes is by playing Fretboard Tetris! Yes, its a bit of a weird concept, but imagine if we break the shapes into two fret coloured micro shapes, the whole thing starts to look a lot like a perfect game of Tetris:

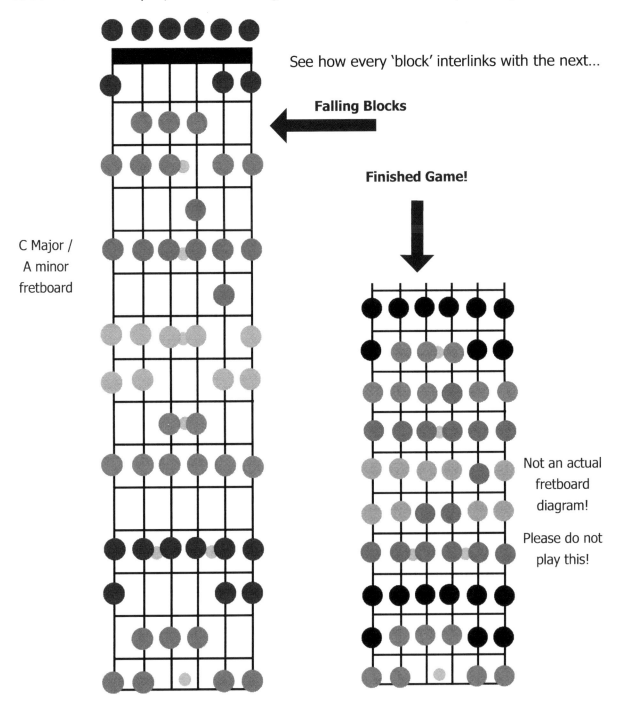

See how every 'block' interlinks with the next...

Falling Blocks

Finished Game!

C Major / A minor fretboard

Not an actual fretboard diagram!

Please do not play this!

Yeah, it's a silly idea, forget I mentioned it!

188

Let's Shred

One way lots of people learn to use these patterns is by utilising string runs and shred patterns. Because these patterns primarily use three note per string ideas it give us access to two traditional positions at once.

Here's a 3 note per string pattern in A minor:

We can also play a similar idea in C Major:

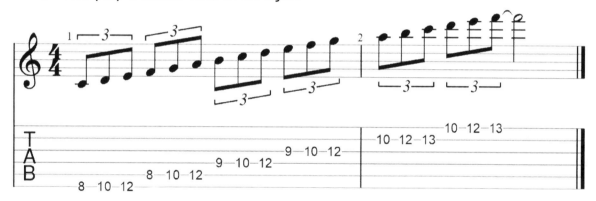

Also remember that if you can think in octaves then you can find repeating patterns where the fingering can stay the same - just move the shape to the next root:

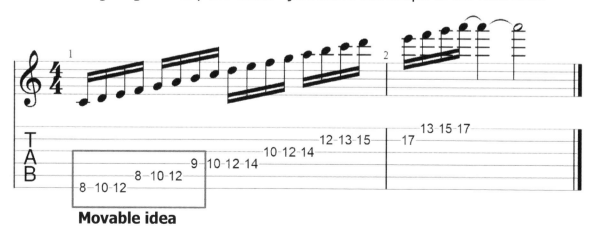

Movable idea

Sequences

Sequences are a lot of fun with full scales:

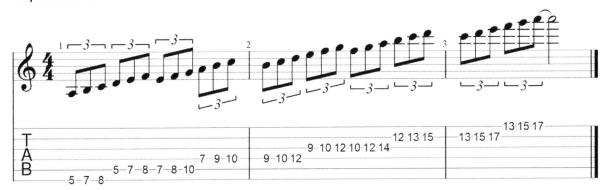

Or take a small idea:

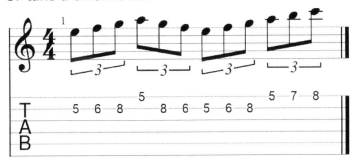

...and grow it in the previous pattern:

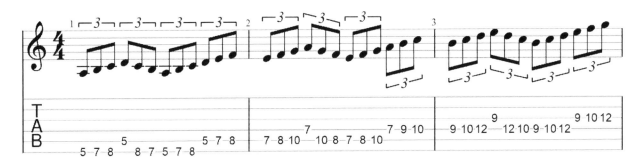

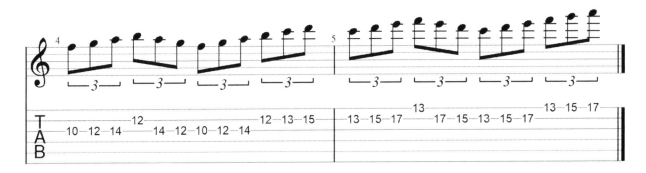

Or try moving up the scale in a linear fashion:

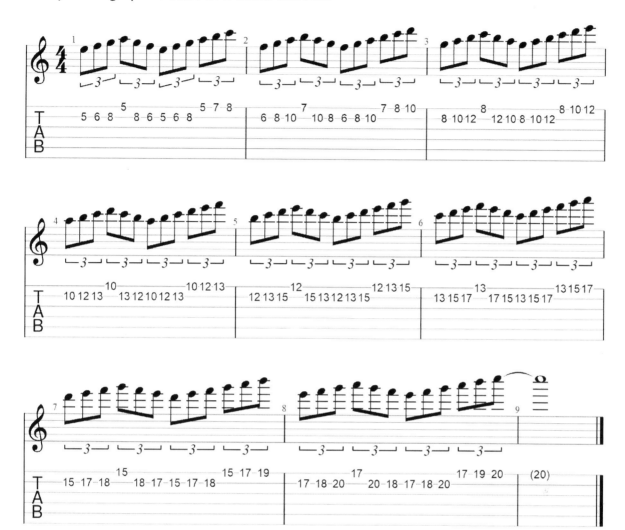

4 notes per string?

In-case 3-notes-per-string isn't quite doing it for you and you need more notes per string or you feel the need to cover even more ground, we can play 4 notes per string! It's not actually any more complex than 3 notes per string as long as you have a good visual command of your fretboard. However, rather than call it 4 notes per string, which does sound like a lot of work and quite off-putting, I actually consider this 3 notes-per-string-with-a-slide.

Here is a one octave C Major scale:

This pattern is worth repeating until you have it smooth. For each note that falls on the same string you can always hammer-on rather than pick, this could help smooth out any bumps.

Here's a 3 octave run using the same technique. You'll notice on the last string we're actually playing a 6 note per string pattern! To do this we slide our 1st finger from 12 - 13th, we then play 15 and 17 with 2nd and 3rd finger, slide 3rd finger to 19 and end on 4th finger on 20th fret.

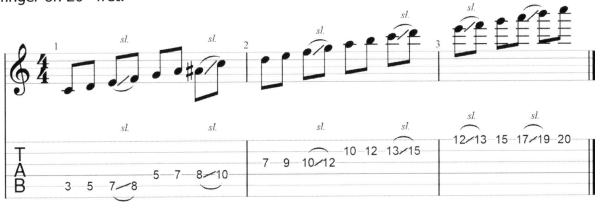

You can decide to navigate your fretboard any way you like, these pattern are just examples. It's worth going back to the fretboard diagram and just playing around to find different ways to move from string to string. You could go 4 notes on one string, 2 on the next followed by 3 notes, generally speaking there really are no rules, you'll always find the next note somewhere handy. Experiment.

WEAVING ARPEGGIOS

Arpeggio's Everywhere

Lets start visualising where all our arpeggio shapes are in this big Major / minor scale too. Lets start with a C Major 7 arpeggio:

C Major 7 5ᵗʰ String root:

Here's a D minor 7 Arpeggio

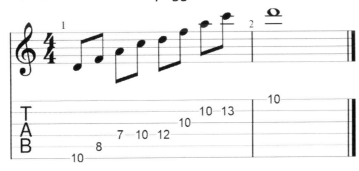

Now look at an E minor 7 Arpeggio:

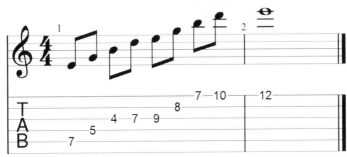

Now look at an E minor 7 Arpeggio:

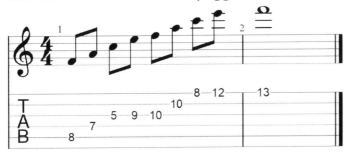

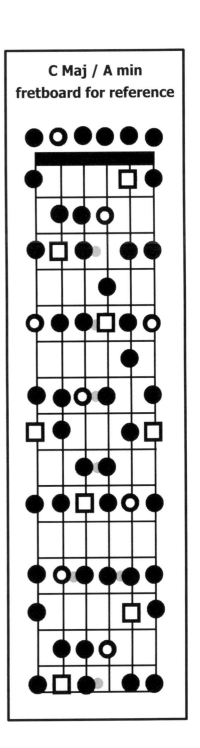

G Dominant 7:

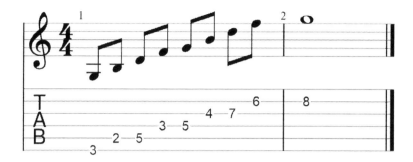

A minor 7:

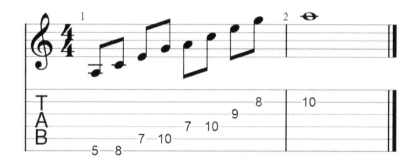

B minor 7b5:

You may have noticed I've purposely written these in positions that spread across the neck rather than just sit over one chord position. This makes them a bit harder to play, but I want you to see how these arpeggios cross into each others territory. This is important.

We know that all of these notes are 'in key' so why can't we play an E minor arpeggio over a C Major chord? Well yeah, you should. Arpeggios aren't just for their equivalent chord you can play them anywhere - give or take your usual ear policing decisions obviously!

Connect the chords

Next I would get used to connecting arpeggio shapes in key. So connect a C Major arpeggio to a D minor arpeggio to an E minor to an F Major to G Major to A minor to B diminished and back to C Major. One example of this might be:

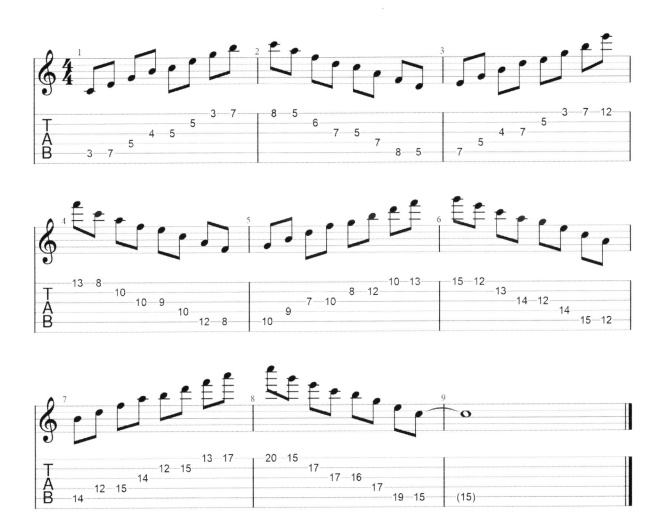

This can be done in any number of ways so experiment. If you get to a note where you can't visualise its arpeggio shape try doing one chord at a time instead. Go back to the CAGED idea on page 134 and link all the positions of one chord together. Start with linking all C Major chords, then all D minors, all E minors etc.

Your aim is to see all these arpeggio options when you are soloing.

Arpeggios over non arpeggio chords!

A couple of pages ago I suggested that you can play arpeggios over chords that aren't of the arpeggio you're playing.

I want to show you some great tonalities that come from such shenanigans:

Record yourself playing a C Major 7 chord. Just the one chord. Add a bit of a groove to it, but for now stick to just that chord.

Next play your C Major 7 arpeggio over it, along with your C Major scale. Get a good ear for how that sounds.

Good. Now play E minor 7 arpeggios over it. You can also increase this arpeggio to a full E minor pentatonic scale if you like. Now, how cool does that sound?

The answer is very cool!

Why it works so well is subject to another book so I won't go into it here, suffice to say that if we examine the E minor 7 arpeggio from the point of view of the C Major scale, we're playing the intervals 3 5 7 and 9 - all the cool chord tones of C Major - put simply, there are no bad notes.

The other nice thing about the E minor 7 arpeggio over C Major is you never actually play a C note. So when played over the C Major chord it never sound quite settled - and every note sounds like an added colour.

This also works in other keys, obviously, the maths stays the same. So in C, the Em arpeggio is the iii arpeggio. So the same effect in G would be the iii of G which would be a Bm arpeggio.

It's worth experimenting with the other arpeggios too, The iii has the best chord tones, but some of the other have interesting colour tones you may like.

Here's a list of 7th arpeggio colour tones when compared to a C Major chord

Dm7 - 9 4 6 R	**Em7** - 3 5 7 9
FM7 - 4 6 R 10	**G7** - 5 7 9 4
Am7 - 6 R 3 5	**Bm7b5** - 7 6 9 4

Stacking Arpeggios

This is really extending arpeggios, but as I'm trying to keep the theory small in this book, we'll look at how mixing these shapes can cause cool sounds.

Take what we just did. The CMaj7 and Em7. Lets join a CM7 arpeggio to an Em and see how that sounds:

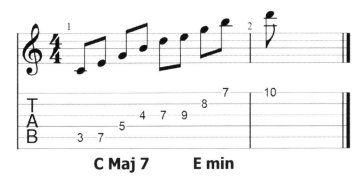

C Maj 7   E min

Really nice! And for all the reasons we've already discussed.

Lets dissect this further for a moment.

We could view this as a C triad followed by a G triad, followed by an Em triad:

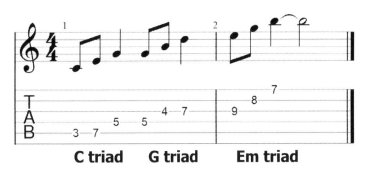

C triad   G triad   Em triad

So, do we want to view it like this? That's up to you, but viewing it like this can help you see how familiar everything actually is and how navigating your fretboard by using arpeggios can be really helpful to finding interesting tones that you wouldn't otherwise have found using your pentatonic boxes.

This last example runs through some arpeggio options in one position, this would work over an Am or C Major chord.

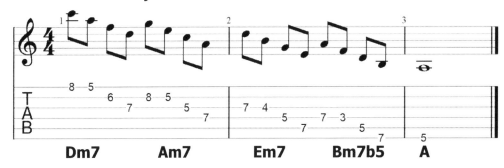

Dm7   Am7   Em7   Bm7b5   A

The Circle of 5ths

Learn the Music

As guitarist, the vast majority of us are still reluctant to 'learn the music' because we're all about the 'feel, man'... However, one part of music theory that is worth learning above all others is the circle of fifths. This is the times tables of music. You know how maths (or 'math' for my American friends) becomes easier once you know your times tables, well, music becomes easier once you've digested the circle of fifths and it's this that is frequently the one concept that, once leaned, will make lots of other music theory seem not quite so bad after all. Let's look at it...

We start with our C Major scale.
We know there are no sharps of flats in it.
We know that its relative minor is A minor.

If we move to the 5th of C we reach G.

We know that G has one Sharp - an F♯.
We also know that its relative minor is E minor.

The 5th of G is D

D has two sharps. We carry over the one from G - the F♯
and add the note before D - a C♯.
Its relative minor, which you should be able to work out from your scale positions is B minor.

The 5th of D is A

A has three sharps, we carry the two over from G (F♯)
and D (C♯) and add the note before A - G♯
It's relative minor is F♯m as discovered on page 84.

C
Am 5th
G
F♯ 5th
Em
D
F♯ C♯
Bm
5th
A
F♯ C♯ G♯
F♯m

That's the first quarter of the circle learned. You will have noticed that the further we go around the more sharps get added to the next key. For a minute lets turn our attention to the opposite side. When we go this way we add flats - ♭. There are two ways you can think of this. We can keep counting 5ths but because we're going the other way you need to count backwards - C B A G F - the next note is F. Or you can count up in 4ths - C D E F - next note is F. I personally count up in 4ths because counting backwards confuses me, but you do whichever feels right for you.

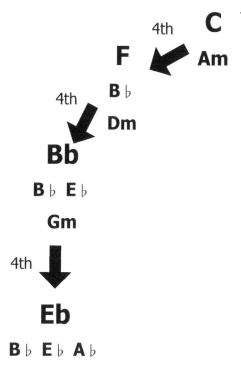

C

4th ← Am

F

B♭

4th Dm

Bb

B♭ E♭

Gm

4th ↓

Eb

B♭ E♭ A♭

Cm

This time we will start at C again but move to the left. Decide whether you want to count up 4ths or backwards 5ths.

Our next key is F

It has one flat - a B♭
It's relative minor is D minor

Move from F brings us to B♭

B♭ has two flats the B♭ and E♭
It's relative minor is G minor

Next 4th or 5th brings us to E♭
E♭ has 3 flats B♭ E♭ and A♭
Its relative minor is C minor

It's probably become apparent by now that when we figure out which flats we have in each key we don't just borrow from the last key but we steal from the next. F steals the B♭, which is the next key. The B♭ keeps its B♭ and steals the E♭ from the next key etc.

First half of Circle of 5ths

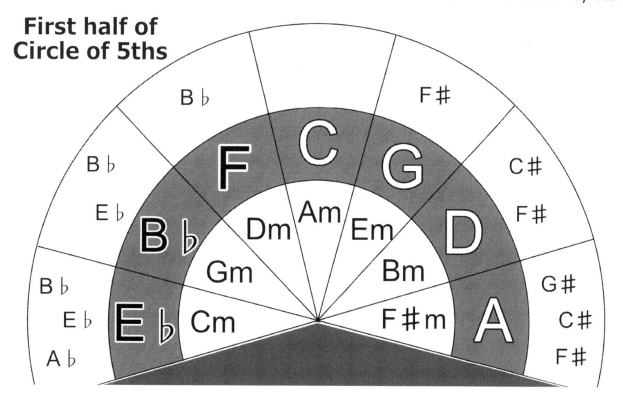

On Guitar

For most of us the circle of 5th's doesn't get much more complicated than this. We need a few more positions on guitar, specifically E is a very popular guitar key, which is the next position around from A. But let's take a quick detour to show you how we can visualise this on guitar.

Lets start at our C and move in 5ths on our fretboard. It looks like this:

Here we've started at our 3rd fret 5th string C. We move up a 5th to G. G has one sharp - the note before it - F#

We can then move up a 5th to D. We take the F# with us and add the note before D - C#

And we can continue this way moving in 5th and collecting our sharps as we go.

As you will see on the full diagram things get more complicated around F# / Gb as we start to cross over en-harmonic notes, so lets stop here.

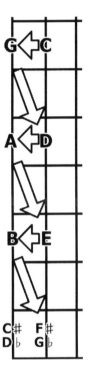

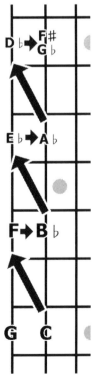

Our b keys work the same but in the opposite direction.

We start with our C again, but this time we need to move a 4th This require us to move backwards across our fretboard, so start up on the 15th Fret C and work backwards from there.
C moves to F, which steals the Bb from the next 4th. We then move the 4th to the Bb and steal the Eb from the next position, you get the idea, and we can continue until we get to the Gb.

Full Circle

As mentioned previously as guitarist we rarely have to think much beyond the top half of the circle plus E. But in case you're interested here's the full circle.

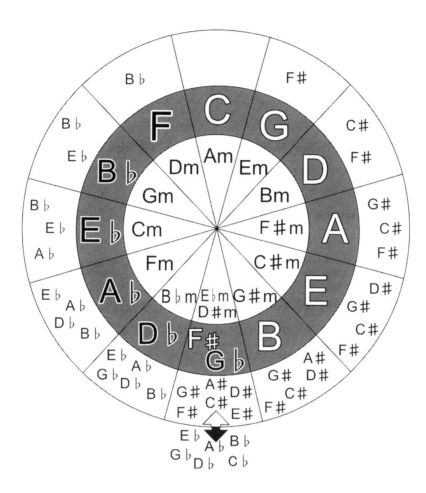

As I said before the cross-over at the bottom gets more complicated because we start to use en-harmonic names for our notes. For instance if you look at the F#/G♭ position you will see that in our flat key we have a C♭, and we know there is no such thing as C♭ because that would be a B right?! Well, not here, because we've already used the designation 'B' for the B♭ we can't use it again for B so instead we have to use C♭. And the same applies for the sharp keys, we have an E# instead of an F and the next position gives us a B#, which is a C - but in this case its not, its a B#! And this only gets worse the further you continue around each side - which is why I've stopped at F#/Gb!

And there's more...

Finding the notes in keys signatures isn't the only use for our circle of 5ths. We can also see our chords in our keys easily too.

If we split the circle into three block sections with your key in the middle in this case C - we can see all of our key chords.:

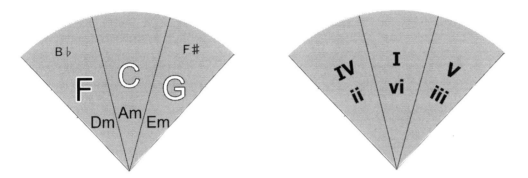

With the exception of our vii (diminished) which, as we know, is the note before the I chord, in this case B, we can see our I ii iii IV V vi chords are C Dm Em F G Am.

Pick another section:

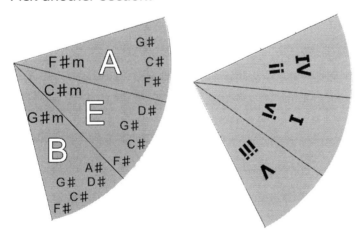

This time we're looking at the Key of E and we can see that our ii is F#m iii is G#m the IV is A, V is B, vi is C#m and the vii will be D#, because it's the note before E.

THE END?

Nope, just the beginning

I have a friend who teaches Tae Kwon Do who once said to me that gaining a black belt isn't the end of their training but just the beginning. That it signifies the start of a lifelong road of self betterment and personal achievement - now they have the tools, it's their turn to put them to good use.

Learning the guitar is the same. I hope this book has given you the tools to navigate the Major and minor scale on your fretboard, understand chords, intervals and harmonies. You now have the capabilities to write songs and create emotions as a part of that knowledge. That's a huge deal.

But it's not the end. The information in this book will enable you to understand the vast majority of music theory in popular music. But there is still more to learn. We haven't touched on modes, harmonic and melodic minor scales, diminished ideas, bigger chord extensions and arpeggios, a wealth of lead guitar technique and much much more.

Well, luckily for you more books in the series are currently underway and will pick up where this one left off!

But right now, you should celebrate finishing this book in a way you consider representative of this achievement, and you have my sincere congratulations for doing so.

Good job!

This

CERTIFICATE OF
AWESOME

Premium Award

is awarded to:

- - - - - - - - - - - - - -

for completing the Guitar Explorium's

Book of Knowledge

The Guitar Explorium

NOTES

Feel free to photocopy this portion of the book

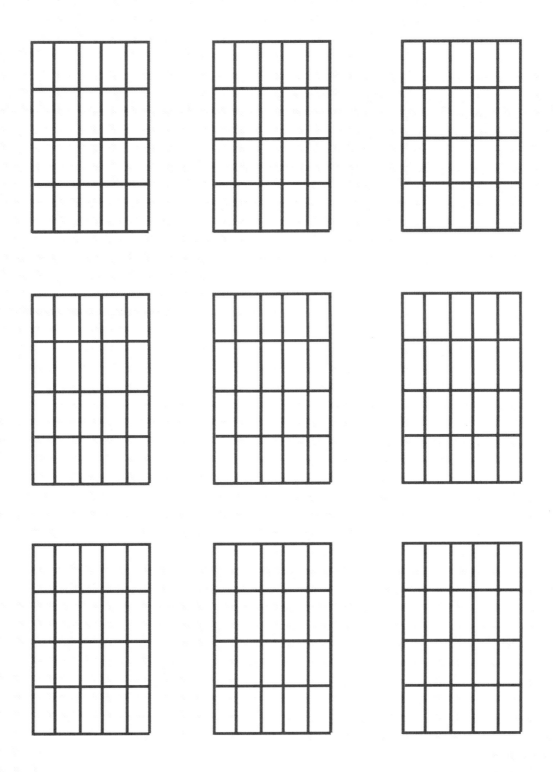

www.theguitarexplorium.com

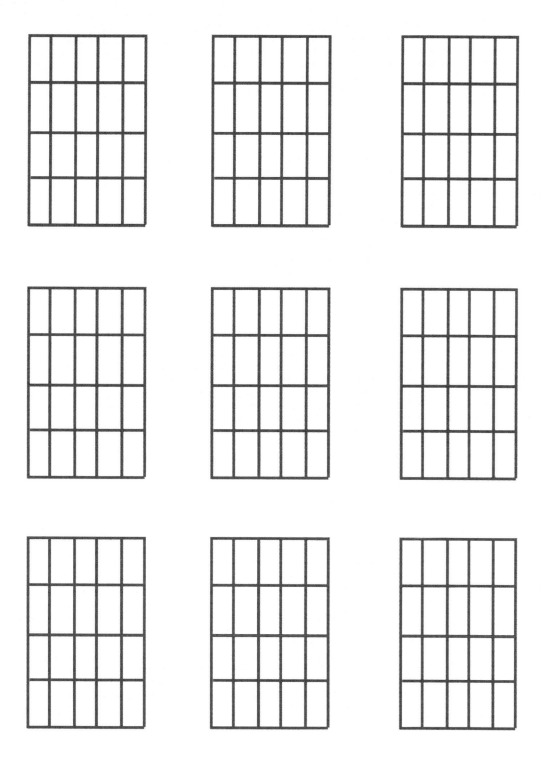

T
A
B

T
A
B

T
A
B

T
A
B

T
A
B

T
A
B

T
A
B

T
A
B

T
A
B

T
A
B

T
A
B

T
A
B

T
A
B

T
A
B

T
A
B

T
A
B

T
A
B

T
A
B

Printed in Great Britain
by Amazon